COLEMAN'S
Songs For Men

The Best New and Old for Men's Voices Largely for Religious Services But Also Many of the Fine Old Plantation Songs and Some of the World's Best Solos, Duets and Other Specials

---

Robert H. Coleman, Compiler
B. B. McKinney, Musical Editor

Published in Round and Shaped Notes

BROADMAN PRESS
Nashville, Tennessee

Foreword

COLEMAN'S SONGS FOR MEN will, we believe, prove a distinct contribution to the increasing demand for *Male Quartets* and Male Chorus work. This book contains what we consider the best songs for men to be found in this country today. In addition to the arrangements which have proven to be most popular, it contains many new songs and new arrangements of old songs, which we are sure will be appreciated. There are also here a number of Old Plantation Melodies for which there is a constant demand. Even aside from Church services, music by men proves very interesting and attractive. The old melodies in this book will be interesting for home enjoyment, for school work or for clubs. Most of this music is very simple and, therefore, can be used by almost any male quartet or chorus. Our prayer is that this book may be a blessing to humanity and an honor to God.

—The Editors.

Printed in the United States of America
Copyrighted 1932 by Robert H. Coleman, Dallas, Texas
10.MH52K

COLEMAN'S SONGS FOR MEN

No. 1 **Hear The Savior's Call.**

Arr. Copyright, 1932, by Robert H. Coleman

Franz Abt. Arr. by B. B. McKinney.

Staccato.

1. Hear the Savior's call, Christians one and all, Hear your Master's earnest cry,
2. Now in Je-sus' name, Who from heaven came To redeem a world from woe,
3. Raise the ban-ner high, Dare to do or die, As a wit-ness for thy God,

Look redeemed band, See the beck'ning hand To the har-vest wav-ing nigh.
Take the mighty word, The all conquering sword To the conflict boldly go.
Tho' be-set by foes, Tho' the world oppose, Keep the path thy Captain trod.

CHORUS.

Sound the word from shore to shore, Till the world shall Christ a-

Sound the word from shore to shore, Till the

dore, Sound the word from shore to shore, Till the world shall Christ adore.

world shall Christ a-dore, shore to shore.

No. 2 Yield Not To Temptation.

Copyright, 1926, by Lorenz Publishing Co, Used by per,

H. R. Palmer. Ernest O. Sellers.

1. Yield not to temp-ta-tion, For yield-ing is sin, Each vic-t'ry will help you Some oth-er to win; Fight man-ful-ly on-ward, Dark pas-sions sub-due, Look ev-er to Je-sus, He will car-ry you through.

2. Shun e-vil com-pan-ions, Bad language dis-dain, God's name hold in rev-'rence, Nor take it in vain; Be thought-ful and earn-est, Kind-heart-ed and true, Look ev-er to Je-sus, He will car-ry you through.

3. To him that o'er-com-eth, God giv-eth a crown, Thro' faith we shall con-quer, Tho' oft-en cast down; He who is our Sav-iour, Our strength will re-new, Look ev-er to Je-sus, He will car-ry you through.

Chorus.

Ask the Saviour to help you, Comfort, strengthen and keep you; He is will-ing to aid you, He will car-ry you through.

No. 3 Wonderful Story Of Love.

Arr. copyright, 1932, by Robert H. Coleman

J. M. D.   Arr. from Driver by B. B. McKinney.

1. Won-der-ful sto-ry of love! Tell it to me a-gain; Won-der-ful sto-ry of love! Wake the im-mor-tal strain! An-gels with rapture an-nounce it, Shepherds with wonder receive it; Sinner, oh! won't you believe it?

2. Won-der-ful sto-ry of love! Tho' you are far a-way; Won-der-ful sto-ry of love! Still He doth call to-day; Call-ing from Cal-va-ry's mountain, Down from the crystal bright fountain, E'en from the dawn of creation,

3. Won-der-ful sto-ry of love! Je-sus provides a rest; Won-der-ful sto-ry of love! For all the pure and blest; Rest in those mansions a-bove us, With those who've gone on before us, Singing the rap-tu-rous cho-rus,

CHORUS.

Won-der-ful sto-ry of love! Won - der - ful! Won - der - ful! Won - der - ful! Wonderful st-ory of love.
Won-der-ful sto-ry of love! Won-der-ful sto-ry of love! Wonderful sto-ry of love!

No. 4 Sweet By And By.

Arr. copyright, 1932, by Robert H. Coleman.

S. F. Bennett. Jas. P. Webster. Arr. by B. B. McKinney.

No. 5   O My Redeemer.

Fanny J. Crosby.   Arr. copyright, 1932, by Robert H. Coleman.   Arr. B. B. McKinney

1. O my Re-deem-er, What a Friend Thou art to me! O what a
2. When, in their beauty, Stars un-veil their sil-ver light, Then, O my
3. Je-sus. my Sav-iour, When the last deep shadows fall; When, in the

Ref-uge I have found in Thee! When the way was drear-y,
Sav-iour, Give me songs at night— Songs of yon-der man-sions,
si-lence I shall hear Thy call,— In Thine arms re-pos-ing,

And my heart was sore op-pressed, 'Twas Thy voice that lulled me
Where the dear ones, gone be-fore, Sing Thy praise for-ev-er,
Let me breathe my life a-way, And a-wake tri-umph-ant,

CHORUS.

To a calm, sweet rest.
On that peace-ful shore. Near-er, draw near-er, Till my soul is
In e-ter-nal day.

lost in Thee; Near-er, draw near-er, Blessed Lord, to me.
Blessed Lord, to me.

No. 6 He'll Keep Me True

J. W. Montgomery.   Copyright, 1932, by Robert H. Coleman.   Haldor Lillenas.

1. I'm trust-ing God for grace and pow'r, He'll ev-er keep me true;
2. His might-y hand thus far has led, He'll ev-er keep me true;
3. Un-til my day of toil is o'er, He'll ev-er keep me true;

I'll lean on Him each day and hour, He'll ev-er keep me true.
His shelt'ring grace o'er me is spread, He'll ev-er keep me true.
Un-til I reach the homeland shore, He'll ev-er keep me true.

CHORUS.

He'll ev-er keep...... me true........ In all I say........ or do;...... I'm trust-ing Him for grace and pow'r, To keep me al-ways true, To keep me al-ways true.
Ev-er keep me, keep me true, all I say or do, or do; Trust-ing Him for grace, for grace and pow'r,

No. 7   He Loves Me Still.

Agnes E. Volentine.   Copyright, 1932, by Robert H. Coleman.   **Haldor Lillenas.**
Melody in first bass throughout.

1. Tho' storms may beat and thunders roll, Temptations sweep a-cross my soul;
2. When sorrow comes, or deep dis-tress, When anxious cares up-on me press;
3. Let rich-es fly and friends de-part, Let cru-el words pierce like a dart;

Yet there is one who has con-trol, And loves me still,.... and loves me still.
When filled the cup of bit-ter-ness, Yet I may know.... He loves me still.
Yet Christ will bind my wounded heart, He loves me still,.... He loves me still.

loves me still,

Chorus.

What-ev-er comes,........ He loves me still,.......... What-ev-er
What-ev-er comes,   He loves me still,

comes...... of good or ill;......... His gracious word...... He will ful-
Whatever comes   of good or ill;   His gracious word

fill,......... He loves me still,........ He loves me still,..........
He will ful-fill,   He loves me still,   He loves me still.

No. 8 Never Alone.

As arranged for and sung by The Bel-Canto Quartet, Dallas, Texas.

E. E. Rexford.   Arr. copyright, 1932, by Robert H. Coleman.   Arr. Lawrence Bolton.

2nd Tenor.

1. The way that leads us heav'n-ward Is oft-en rough and steep;
2. Then, think-ing of the bur - den He bore up Cal-v'ry's Hill,
3. Take cour-age, way-worn pil - grim! Tho' mists and shad-ows hide

We strug-gle in the dark - ness, And some-times pause to weep;
We cease our weak com-plain - ing, Our lips, for shame, are still;
The face of Christ who loves thee, He's ev - er at thy side;

Then comes a thought to com - fort The heart, dis-cour-aged grown,
And hearts that pain has tor - tured For - get to make their moan.
Reach out thy hand to find Him, And lo! the mists have flown—

He who trod Cal-v'ry's pathway Nev - er will leave thee a - lone.
Re-mem-b'ring Him who prom-ised Nev - er to leave us a - lone.
He smiles, and whis-pers soft - ly, Nev - er to leave thee a - lone.

D.S.—He prom-ised never to leave thee, Nev - er to leave thee a - lone.

CHORUS.

No, nev - er a - lone, (a - lone,) No nev - er a - lone!

No. 9   Lead Me Gently Home, Father.

As arranged for and sung by The Bel-Canto Quartet, Dallas, Texas.

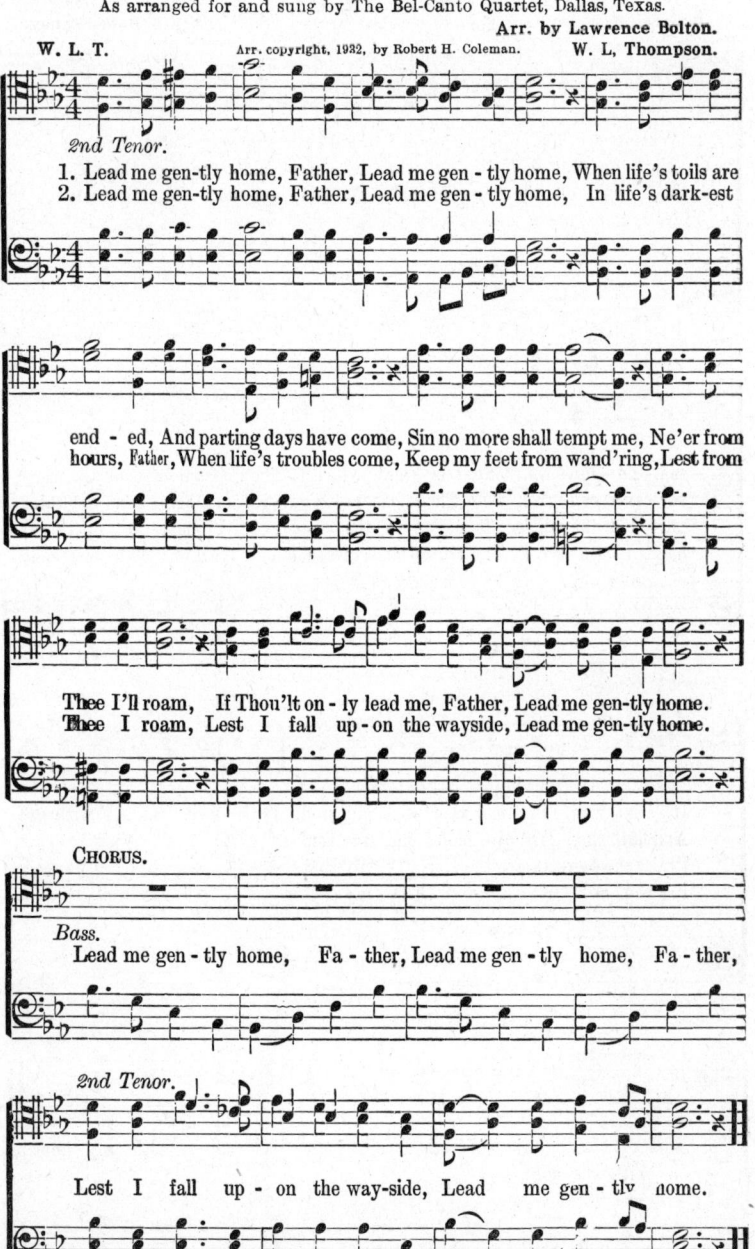

W. L. T.   Arr. copyright, 1932, by Robert H. Coleman.   Arr. by Lawrence Bolton.   W. L. Thompson.

2nd Tenor.

1. Lead me gen-tly home, Father, Lead me gen - tly home, When life's toils are
2. Lead me gen-tly home, Father, Lead me gen - tly home, In life's dark-est

end - ed, And parting days have come, Sin no more shall tempt me, Ne'er from
hours, Father, When life's troubles come, Keep my feet from wand'ring, Lest from

Thee I'll roam, If Thou'lt on - ly lead me, Father, Lead me gen-tly home.
Thee I roam, Lest I fall up - on the wayside, Lead me gen-tly home.

Chorus.

Bass.

Lead me gen - tly home, Fa - ther, Lead me gen - tly home, Fa - ther,

2nd Tenor.

Lest I fall up - on the way-side, Lead me gen - tly home.

No. 10   It Is Well With My Soul.

H. G. Spafford.   Copyright, 1904, by The John Church Co.   P. P. Bliss.
Arr. B. B. McKinney.

1. When peace, like a riv-er at-tend-eth my way, When sor-rows like
2. Tho' Sa-tan should buf-fet, tho' tri-als should come, Let this blest as-
3. My sin— oh, the bliss of this glo-ri-ous tho't—My sin—not in
4. And, Lord, haste the day when the faith shall be sight, The clouds be rolled

sea - bil - lows roll; What-ev - er my lot, Thou hast taught me to say,
sur - ance con - trol, That Christ has re - gard - ed my help - less es - tate,
part, but the whole, Is nailed to the cross and I bear it no more,
back as a scroll, The trump shall re-sound and the Lord shall de-scend,

CHORUS.

It is well, it is well with my soul. It is well........ with my
And hath shed His own blood for my soul.
Praise the Lord, praise the Lord, O my soul.
"E - ven so"—it is well with my soul.   it is well

soul,.......... It is well, it is well with my soul.
with my soul,

No. 11 Never Grow Old.

Jas. C. M. Owned by Jas. C. Moore

Jas. C. Moore.
Arr. by B. B. McKinney.

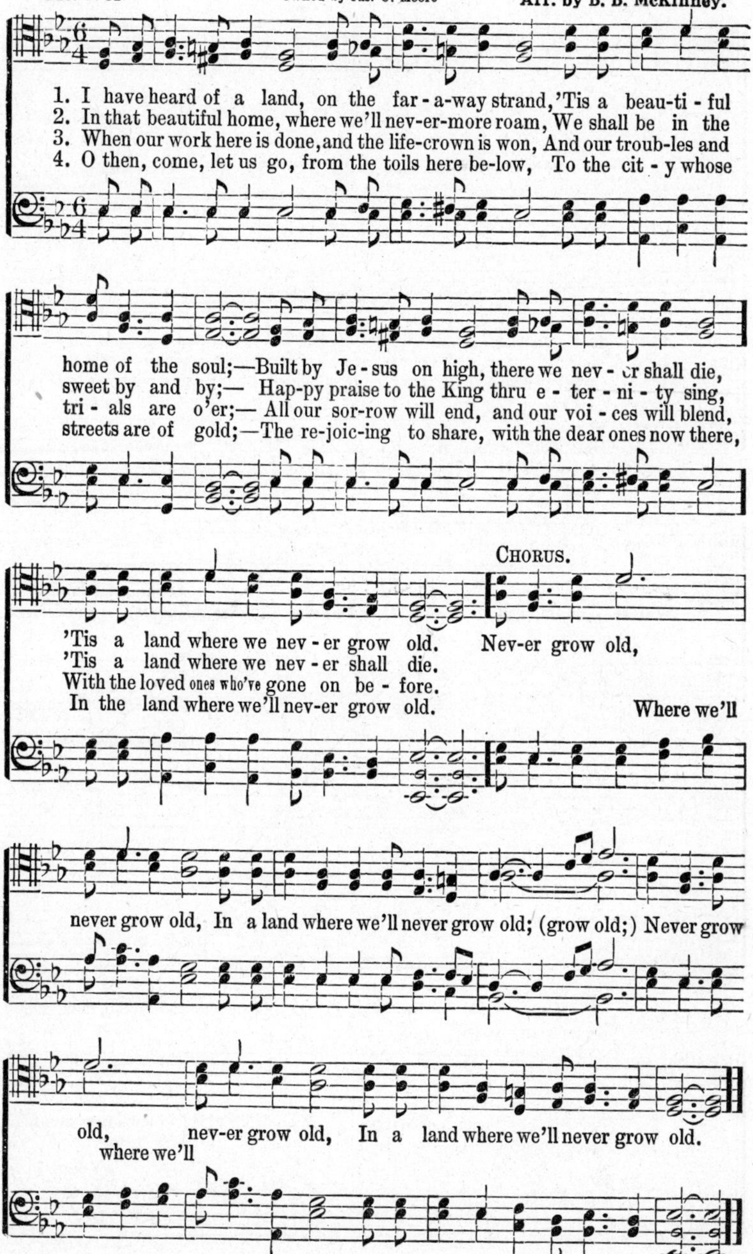

No. 12 Wandering Child, O Come Home.

K. G. B.
Moderato.

Copyright, 1914, by Homer A. Rodeheaver.
International copyright secured.

Kem G. Bottorf.

1. Have you wandered a-way from your Fa-ther's care, Heav-y heart-ed and sad do you roam? There's a sweet, gen-tle voice call-ing now to you—
2. Is your frail bark a-drift on life's rag-ing sea, Are you tossed on its bil-lows and foam? There's a safe har-bor home, waiting now for you—
3. He is plead-ing to-day, heed His gen-tle voice, As He bids you no long-er to roam, To that dear Father's house haste without de-lay—

CHORUS. *pp Second time.*

Wand'ring child, wand'ring child, O come home. Child, come home, Child, come home, child, come home, child, come home, Wand'ring child, why long-er roam? Wand'ring child, why long-er roam? 'Tis thy Wand'ring child, O come home, come home.

'Tis thy Fa-ther now entreats— Wand'ring child, come home, come home.
Fa-ther en-treats— Wand'ring child, O come home.

No. 13   May God Depend On You?

Copyright, 1906, by the Lorenz Publishing Co.

W. C. Martin.   Ira B. Wilson.

1. In the war-fare that is rag-ing For the truth and for the right,
2. See, they come on sa-ble pin-ions. Come they in Sa-tan-ic might,—
3. From His throne the Fa-ther sees us; An-gels help us to pre-vail;

When the con-flict, fierce, is rag-ing With the pow-ers of the night,
Pow-ers come and dark do-min-ions From the re-gions of the night,
And our lead-er true is Je-sus, And we shall not, can-not fail,

God needs peo-ple brave and true;   May He then de-pend on you?
God requires the brave and true: May He now de-pend on you?
Triumph crowns the brave and true,— May the Lord de-pend on you?
     peo - ple   brave and true;

CHORUS.

May the Lord.... depend on you?... Loy-al-ty..... is but His due;...
May the Lord de - pend on you?   Loy-al-ty is but His due;

Say, O spir-it brave and true,   That He may de-pend on you.
    spir - it   brave and true,

No. 14 **He Lives On High.**

Words and arr. copyright, 1921, by Robert H. Coleman.

B. B. McK.

Arr. by B. B. McKinney.
From Hawaiian Folk Song.

1. Christ the Savior came from heaven's glory, To redeem the lost from sin and shame, On His brow He wore the thorn-crown gory, And upon Calvary He took my blame.
2. He arose from death and all its sorrow, To dwell in that land of joy and love; He is coming back some glad tomorrow, And He'll take all His children home above.
3. Weary soul, to Jesus come confessing, Redemption from sin He offers thee; Look to Jesus and receive a blessing, There is life, there is joy and victory.

CHORUS.

He lives on high, He lives on high, Triumphant over sin and all its stain; He lives on high, He lives on high, Some day He's coming again.

No. 15 Sunset Hour.

Copyright, 1928, by Robert H. Coleman
International copyright secured.

E. C. Baird. B. B. McKinney.

No. 16   **Memories of Galilee.**

Dr. R. Morris   H. R. Palmer, owner of copyright. Used by permission.   H. R. Palmer.

1. Each coo-ing dove, ... and sigh-ing bough .... That makes the
2. Each flow-'ry glen .... and mos-sy dell, ... Where hap-py
3. And when I read .... the thrilling lore, ... Of Him who

eve .... so blest to me, ... Has something
birds .... in song a-gree, ... Thro' sun-ny
walked .... up-on the sea, ... I long, O

far .... di-vin-er now, ... It bears me back .... to
morn .... the praises tell, ... Of sights and sounds .... in
how .... I long once more .... To fol-low Him .... in

REFRAIN.

Gal-i-lee............. O Gal-i-lee, sweet Gal-i-lee, Where Jesus loved so
to Gal-i-lee.

much to be, O Gal-i-lee, Blue Gal-i-lee, Come sing thy song again to me.

No. 17

Calvary.

W. McK. Darwood.
Copyright, 1886, by Jno. R. Sweney.
Jno. R. Sweney.
Arr. for men by B. B. McKinney.

1. On Calv'ry's brow........ my Sav-iour died,........ 'Twas their my
2. 'Mid rending rocks.......... and dark'ning skies, ... My Sav-iour
3. O Je-sus Lord............how can it be,...........That Thou shouldst

1. On Calv'y's brow   my Saviour died,

Lord.......... was cru-ci-fied; ....'Twas on the cross.......... He
bows........... His head and dies;.......... The op'ning vail........... re-
give .... Thy life for me, ... To bear the cross........ and

'Twas there my Lord   was cru-ci-fied;   'Twas on the cross

bled for me,............. And purchased there.......... my pardon free.
veals the way,........... To heav-en's joys .... and endless day.
ag-o-ny, ... In that dread hour .... on Cal-va-ry.

He bled for me,   And purchased there

CHORUS.

O Cal-va-ry! dark Cal-va-ry! Where Je-sus shed His blood for me, (for me;)

rit.

O Cal-va-ry! blest Cal-va-ry! 'Twas there my Sav-iour died for me.

No. 18. Go Through The Gates.

Jennie Wilson. Copyright, 1906, by the Lorenz Publishing Co. Ira B. Wilson.

1. Go thro' the gates, O church of Christ, Cast up, cast up a safe high-way;
2. Prepare the way of ho-li-ness, Remove the stones that wound the feet,
3. Go thro' the gates, make known the strength That cometh from a faith di-vine,

For all the peo-ple make a road, That from the kingdom none need stay.
That all who walk there-in may find A joy and bless-ing pure and sweet.
A-rise, a-rise, O church of Christ, Be true and vic-t'ry shall be thine.

CHORUS.

Go thro' the gates, ... O church of Christ, ...
Go thro the gates,   O church of Christ,   And

And   lift the roy-al standard high;   The sav-ing pow'r
lift the roy-al standard high; .... The saving pow'r ....

of Je-sus tell .... E're wait-ing peo-ple faint and die.

No. 19   Gathering Home.

Mrs. Mariana B. Slade.
Arr. copyright 1925, by Rob't H. Coleman.
R. M. McIntosh.
Arr. B. B. McK.

1. Up to the boun-ti-ful Giv-er of life,—Gathering home! gath-er-ing home!
2. Up to the city where falleth no night,—Gathering home! gath-er-ing home!
3. Up to the beautiful mansions a-bove,—Gathering home! gath-er-ing home!

Up to the dwelling where cometh no strife, The dear ones are gath-er-ing home.
Up where the Savior's own face is the light, The dear ones are gath-er-ing home.
Safe in the arms of His in-fi-nite love, The dear ones are gath-er-ing home.

Chorus.

Gath-er-ing home!............ gath-er-ing home!...............
    Gath-er-ing home!   gath-er-ing home!

Nev-er to sor-row more, nev-er to roam; Gath-er-ing home!............
    Gath-er-ing home!

gath-er-ing home!............ God's children are gath-er-ing home.
    gath-er-ing home!

No. 20 A Friend To Man.

Adapted by B. B. McK. Copyright 1925, by Rob't H. Coleman. B. B. McKinney.

1. Let me trav-el the road, the road of life, Where the rac-es of men press on, The men who are weak from their load of sin, And the men who are good and strong, I would not look with a scor-ner's eye, Nor hurl the cyn-ic's ban, Let me trav-el the road, the road of life, And be a friend to man.

2. Let me see as I trav-el up-on my way, On the great high-way of life, The men who press on with the ar-dor of hope, And the men who are faint with strife, Let me turn not a-way from their smiles and tears, Both part of an all-wise plan, Let me trav-el the road, the road of life, And be a friend to man.

3. Let me trav-el the road, the road of life, Where some sin-burdened soul I'll meet, Let me be a balm to his ach-ing heart, And a guide to his way-ward feet, Let me tell him of Christ who has died to save, Let me give him sal-va-tion's plan, Let me trav-el the road, the road of life, And be a friend to man.

No. 21 **When They Ring the Golden Bells.**

Dion De Marbelle.
Arr. copyright 1925, by Rob't H. Coleman. Arr. B. B. McKinney.

1. There's a land be-yond the riv-er, That we call the sweet for-ev-er, And we
2. We shall know no sin or sor-row, In that ha-ven of tomorrow, When our
3. When our days shall know their number, And in death we sweetly slumber, When the

on-ly reach that shore by faith's decree; One by one we'll gain the portals, There to
barque shall sail beyond the silver sea; We shall on-ly know the blessing Of our
King commands the spirit to be free; Nev-er-more with anguish la-den, We shall

dwell with the im-mor-tals, When they ring the gold-en bells for you and me.
Fa-ther's sweet ca-ress-ing, When they ring the gold-en bells for you and me.
reach that love-ly ai-den, When they ring the gold-en bells for you and me.

yond the shin-ing riv-er, When they ring the gold-en bells for you and me.

CHORUS.
Don't you hear the bells now ringing? Don't you here the angels singing? 'Tis the glo-ry

hal-le-lu-jah Ju-bi-lee. (Ju-bi-lee.) In that far-off sweet for-ev-er, Just be-

No. 22 — Will You Come?

Anon.
Copyright 1909, by Ernest O. Sellers.
E. O. Sellers.

1. We are trav'ling home to heav'n above, Will you come?........ Will you come?
2. We are going to see the Bleeding Lamb,
3. We are going to join the heav'nly choir, Will you come?

To sing the Sav-iour's dy-ing love, Will you come? Will you come?
In rapt-'rous strains to praise His name, Will you come? Will you come?
To raise our voice and tune the lyre, Will you come? Will you come?

Mil-lions have reached that blest a-bode, A-noint-ed kings and priests to God, And
The crown of life we there shall wear, The conq'rors palm our hands shall bear, And
There saints and an-gels glad-ly sing, Ho-san-nas to their God and King, And

rit.

mil-lions more are on the road; Will you come?........ Will you come?
all the joys of heav'n we'll share,
make the heav'nly ar-ches ring; Will you come?

No. 23 Though Your Sins Be As Scarlet.

Fanny J. Crosby. Copyright preperty of W. H. Doane. W. H. Doane.

Duet or Trio.

1. "Tho' your sins be as scar-let, They shall be as white as snow; as snow;
2. Hear the voice that entreats you, Oh, re-turn ye un - to God! to God!
3. He'll for-give your transgressions, And remember them no more; no more;

Quartet.

Tho' they be red (Tho' they be red) like crim-son, They shall be as wool;"
He is of great (He is of great) com-pas-sion, And of won-drous love;
"Look un - to Me (Look un - to Me,) ye peo - ple," Saith the Lord your God!

Trio. **Quartet.**

"Tho' your sins be as scar - let, Tho' your sins be as scar-let,
Hear the voice that en-treats you, Hear the voice that entreats you;
He'll for - give your trans-gres-sions, He'll for-give your transgressions,

They shall be as white as snow, They shall be as white as snow."
Oh, re - turn ye un - to God! Oh, re - turn ye un - to God!
And re - mem - ber them no more, And re - mem - ber them no more.

No. 24 Is Jesus To Me.

Mrs. W. M. Runyan.   Copyright, 1932, by Robert H. Coleman.   Mrs. J. H. Cassidy.

1. All that my soul in its sin can need, All that my
2. My on-ly claim for all sin for-giv'n, Ground for my
3. Bread for the soul when I hun-ger sore, Grace for my
4. More than my song can in love de-clare, More than all

faith in its pray'r can plead; Cen-ter of life and soul
hope of a home in heav'n; Pow-er thro' which my chains
heart when I thirst for more; Shelt-er-ing Rock when the
meas-ure of praise or pray'r; Com-fort and balm for all

CHORUS.

of my creed Is Je-sus to me.
are riv-en Is Je-sus to me.
storms do roar Is Je-sus to me. He is my Rock in a
of my care Is Je-sus to me.

wea-ry land, He is my Spring 'midst the des-ert sand; Strength

rit.

in my weak-ness that I may stand, Is Je-sus to me.

No. 25 He's Able To Keep You From Falling.

B. B. McKinney.   Copyright, 1932, by Robert H. Coleman.   B. B. McKinney.

1. He's a-ble to keep you from fall-ing, Christ Je-sus who con-quered the grave; He's a-ble to keep you from fall-ing, The One who has pow-er to save. He's a - - - ble to keep you, To keep you from fall-ing; He's a-ble to save to the ut-ter-most, All those who will come un-to Him.

2. He's a-ble to keep you from fall-ing, This prom-ise e-ter-nal is thine; He's a-ble to keep you from fall-ing, Oh bless-ed as-sur-ance di-vine.

3. He's a-ble to keep you from fall-ing, Though Sa-tan may oft-en al-lure; He's a-ble to keep you from fall-ing, Your an-chor in Him is se-cure.

4. He's a-ble to keep you from fall-ing, In heav-en your name's writ-ten down; Be-fore Him you'll stand at His call-ing, An heir to a robe and a crown. He's a-ble, He's a-ble to keep you, To keep you, to keep you from fall-ing;

Chorus.

No. 26 Where We'll Never Grow Old.

Rev. W. W. Bailey.
Arr. copyright, 1932, by Robert H. Coleman.
Arr. by B. B. McKinney.
from I. N. McHose.

1. Oh, have you not heard of that coun-try a-bove, The name of its King and His in-fi-nite love? His chil-dren are death-less and hap-py I'm told; Oh, will it a-bide—will we nev-er grow old?
2. A man-sion of won-der-ful beau-ty is there. And Je-sus that man-sion has gone to pre-pare; Its bright jas-per walls how I long to be-hold, And join in the song that will nev-er grow old.
3. They tell me its friendships and love is so pure, Its joys nev-er die, and its treas-ures are sure; And loved ones de-part-ed, so si-lent and cold, Will greet us a-gain where we'll nev-er grow old.
4. In life's wea-ry con-flicts, there's fainting and care, Each year the gray deep-ens a shade in the hair; But in the blest book where my name is en-rolled, I read of that land where we'll nev-er grow old.

D. S.—To think of that land where we'll nev-er grow old.

CHORUS.

'Twill al-ways be new, it will nev-er de-cay, No night ev-er comes, it will always be day; It gladdens my heart with a joy that's untold,

No. 27   'Twas Jesus' Blood.

R. H. Coleman.   Copyright, 1932, by Robert H. Coleman.   Mrs. J. H. Cassidy.

1. 'Twas Je-sus' blood that bought me, When I was bound by sin; 'Twas Je-sus' love that sought me, When I was vile with-in. Oh, praise Him for a-ton-ing grace, That reached a child of sin-ful race.
2. He prayed there in the gar-den, "Thy will, not mine be done;" Sweat blood-drops for my par-don, In ag-o-ny a-lone. Great joy wells up with-in my soul, Re-deem-ing blood hath made me whole.
3. He bore my sins and sor-rows, On Cal-v'ry's rug-ged hill; And there 'neath earth's dark shadows, Faced death by His own will. To Je-sus Christ my love I give, He gave His life that I might live.
4. I praise Him for re-demp-tion, My song 'twill ev-er be; Blest Lord of all cre-a-tion! His blood a-toned for me. Thro' all His courts my joy shall sound, That I, the lost, by Christ was found.

CHORUS.

'Twas Je-sus' blood a-toned for me, He saved my soul, He set me free; A sin-ner saved proclaims His grace, And in His service seeks a place.

No. 28 I Shall Not Die.

T. O. Chisholm
Copyright, 1932, by Robert H Coleman.
Haldor Lillenas

1. I need not die, an-oth-er died And met the law's demands for me;
2. I need not die, can it be true That He would die while I go free?
3. 'Tis Je-sus Christ, the sinner's Friend, Behold His garments stained with blood;
4. O love tran-scend-ing human thought! O glorious mys-ter-y of grace!

He bore my pen-al-ty for sin "In His own bod-y on the tree."
O tell me, tell me who is this That showed such wondrous love to me?
Who chose a sin-ner's death to die, That He might bring us back to God.
That Christ, the sin-less Son of God Would take the guil-ty sin-ner's place.

Chorus.

I need not die, I shall not die, Tho' death my
I need not die, I shall not die,

por-tion must have been; there's a cross that
For there's a cross........ that stands be-

rit.

stands be-tween ran-somed soul
tween........ My ran-somed soul........ and all my sin.

No. 29   When I See The Blood.

John   Arr. copyright, 1932, by E. O. Sellers.   Ernest O. Sellers.

1. Christ our Redeemer died on the cross, Died for the sinner,
2. Chiefest of sinners Jesus can save, As He has promised,
3. Judgment is coming, all will be there, Who have rejected,
4. Oh, what compassion, oh, boundless love! Jesus hath power,

paid all his due; All who receive Him need never fear, Yes, He will
so will He do; Oh, sinner, hear Him, trust in His word, Then He will
who have refused; Oh, sinner, hasten, let Jesus in, Then God will
Jesus is true; All who believe are safe from the storm, Oh, He will

CHORUS.

pass, will pass over you. When I see the blood, When I see the blood,
When I see the blood, When I see the
When I see the blood, When I
blood, see the blood, I will pass, I will pass over you..........
ov-er you.

No. 30   It Came Upon The Midnight Clear.

Edmund H. Sears.   Arr. copyright 1925, by Rob't H. Coleman.   Arr. B. B. McKinney.

1. It came up-on the mid-night clear, That glorious song of old,
2. Still thro' the clo-ven skies they come, With peaceful wings un-furled.
3. And ye, beneath life's crush-ing load, Whose forms are bend-ing low,
4. For lo, the days are hast-'ning on, By proph-et bards for-told,

From an-gels bend-ing near the earth To touch their harps of gold:
And still their heav'n-ly mu-sic floats O'er all the wea-ry world:
Who toil a-long the climb-ing way With pain-ful steps and slow,—
When with the ev-er-cir-cling years Comes round the age of gold;

"Peace on the earth, good will to men From heav'n's all-gra-cious King."
A-bove its sad and low-ly plains They bend on hov-'ring wing,
Look now! for glad and golden hours Come swift-ly on the wing;
When peace shall o-ver all the earth Its an-cient splen-dors fling,

The world in sol-emn still-ness lay, To hear the an-gels sing.
And ev-er o'er its Ba-bel-sounds The bless-ed an-gels sing.
O rest be-side the wea-ry road, And hear the an-gels sing.
And the whole world give back the song Which now the an-gels sing.

No. 31 Roll, Billows, Roll!

Copyright, 1914, by Hunt and Scholfield.
Owned by Robert H. Coleman.

J. P. S.
J. P. Scholfield.
Arr. I. E. R.

1. I am held by God's right hand, Roll, bil-lows, roll! I fear naught on sea or land, so Roll, bil-lows, roll.
2. What care I for rock or shoal? Roll, bil-lows, roll! All God's host sur-round my soul, so Roll, bil-lows, roll.
3. Tho' what Sa-tan should as-sail, Roll, bil-lows, roll! In God's might I shall pre-vail, so Roll, bil-lows, roll.
4. Oh, that you, my friend, could say, "Roll bil-lows, roll! Christ is keeping me each day, so Roll, bil-lows, roll."

CHORUS.

Roll, bil-lows, roll! Je-sus is my an-chor and He'll keep my soul from ev-'ry foe; So roll, bil-bows, roll!..... Roll, bil-lows, roll!..... Je-sus is my an-chor and He'll keep my soul.

SM-2

No. 32 — The Old Rugged Cross.

Copyright, 1913, by Geo. Bennard.
Homer A. Rodeheaver, owner.

G. B. Rev. Geo. Bennard.

1. On a hill far a-way stood an old rug-ged cross, The em-blem of suf-f'ring and shame; And I love that old cross where the dearest and best For a world of lost sin-ners was slain.
2. Oh, that old rug-ged cross, so despised by the world, Has a wondrous at-trac-tion for me; For the dear Lamb of God left His glo-ry a-bove, To bear it to dark Cal-va-ry.
3. In the old rug-ged cross, stained with blood so divine, A won-drous beau-ty I see; For 'twas on that old cross Je-sus suf-fered and died, To par-don and sanc-ti-fy me.
4. To the old rug-ged cross I will ev-er be true, Its shame and re-proach glad-ly bear; Then He'll call me some day to my home far a-way, Where His glory for-ev-er I'll share.

CHORUS.

So I'll cher-ish the old rug-ged cross, the old rug-ged cross,...... Till my trophies at last I lay down; I will cling to the old rug-ged cross, the old rug-ged cross,......... And exchange it some day for a crown.

No. 33   **The Riches Of Love.**

Rev. H. B. Hartzler.   Copyright, 1916, by D. B. Towner. Renewal.   N. B. Sargent. Arr.
Hope Publishing Co., Owner.

1. The treas-ures of earth are not mine, I hold not its sil-ver and gold; But a treas-ure far great-er is mine; I have rich-es of val-ue un-told.
2. The treas-ures of earth must all fail, Its rich-es and hon-or de-cay, But the rich-es of love that are mine, E-ven death can-not take them a-way.
3. Compared with the rich-es of love, The wealth of the world is but dross; I will seek but Christ Je-sus to win, And for Him I count all things but loss.
3. Come, take of the rich-es of Christ, Ex-haust-less and free is the store; Of its won-der-ful full-ness re-ceive, Till you hun-ger and thirst nev-er-more.

CHORUS.

Oh, the depth of the rich-es of love,........ The rich-es of love, the rich-es of love, in Christ Je-sus, Far bet-ter than gold, or wealth un-told, Are the rich-es of love in Christ Je-sus.

No. 34 Under His Wings.

Words adapted by B. B. Mc.K.
Copyright, 1928, by Robart H. Coleman. International copyright secured.
B. B. McKinney.

1. In God I have found a re-treat, Where I can se-cure-ly a-bide; No ref-uge nor rest so com-plete,
2. I dread not the ter-ror by night, No ar-row can harm me by day; His shad-ow has cov-ered me quite,
3. The wast-ing de-struc-tion at noon, No fear-ful fore-bod-ing can bring; With Je-sus, my soul doth com-mune,
4. A thous-and may fall at my side, Ten thous-and up-on my right hand; A-bove me His wings are spread wide,

And here I shall ev-er re-side.
My fears He has driv-en a-way.
His per-fect sal-va-tion I sing.
Be-neath them in safe-ty I stand.

CHORUS.

Un-der His wings, Un-der His shel-ter-ing wings; What com-fort it brings, My soul glad-ly sings, I'm un-der His shel-ter-ing wings.

No. 35 Wonderful Jesus.

Gypsy Smith's Campaign Song.

Anna B. Russell. Copyright, 1921, by Ernest O. Sellers. Ernest O. Sellers.

Melody in First Tenor.

1. There is nev-er a day so drear-y, There is nev-er a night so long, (so long,) But the soul that is trust-ing Je-sus Will somewhere find a song.
2. There is nev-er a cross so heav-y, There is nev-er a weight of woe, (of woe,) But that Je-sus will help to car-ry, Be-cause He lov-eth so.
3. There is nev-er a care or bur-den, There is nev-er a grief or loss, (or loss,) But that Je-sus in love will light-en, When car-ried to the cross.
4. There is nev-er a guilt-y sin-ner, There is nev-er a wan-d'ring one, (not one,) But that God can in mer-cy par-don, Thro' Je-sus Christ, His Son.

REFRAIN.

Won-der-ful, won-der-ful Je-sus, In the heart He im-plant-eth a song;......... A song of de-im-plant-eth a song; liv'rance of courage and strength, In the heart He implanteth a song.

Deliberately.

No. 36 Onward, Christian Soldiers.

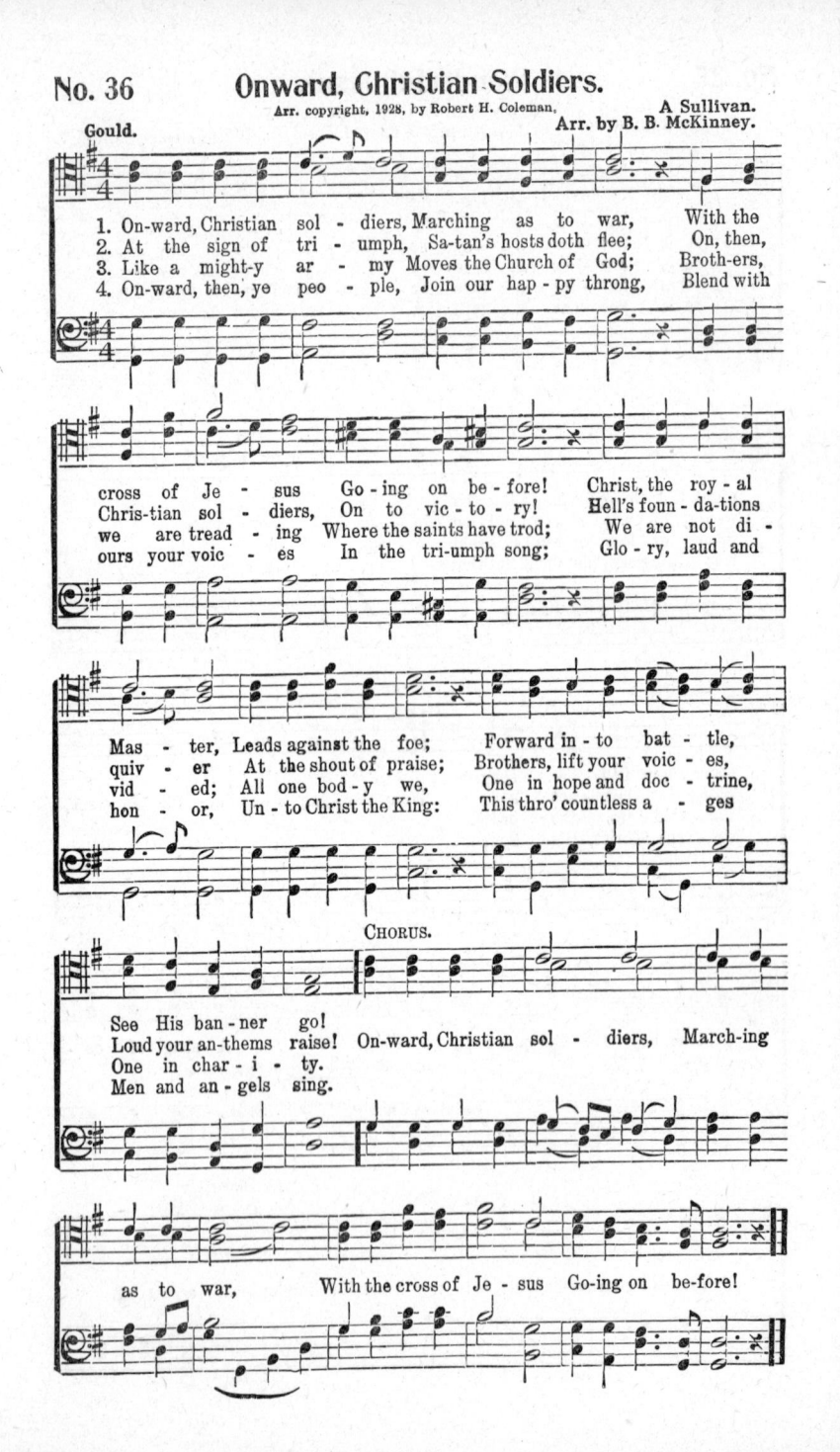

Arr. copyright, 1928, by Robert H. Coleman.

Gould.
Arr. by B. B. McKinney.
A Sullivan.

1. On-ward, Christian sol - diers, Marching as to war, With the cross of Je - sus Go-ing on be - fore! Christ, the roy - al Mas - ter, Leads against the foe; Forward in - to bat - tle, See His ban - ner go!
2. At the sign of tri - umph, Sa-tan's hosts doth flee; On, then, Chris-tian sol - diers, On to vic - to - ry! Hell's foun - da-tions quiv - er At the shout of praise; Brothers, lift your voic - es, Loud your an-thems raise!
3. Like a might-y ar - my Moves the Church of God; Broth-ers, we are tread - ing Where the saints have trod; We are not di - vid - ed; All one bod - y we, One in hope and doc - trine, One in char - i - ty.
4. On-ward, then, ye peo - ple, Join our hap - py throng, Blend with ours your voic - es In the tri-umph song; Glo - ry, laud and hon - or, Un - to Christ the King: This thro' countless a - ges Men and an - gels sing.

Chorus.

On-ward, Christian sol - diers, March-ing as to war, With the cross of Je - sus Go-ing on be - fore!

No. 37 Day Is Dying In The West.

Mary A. Lathbury.   Arr. copyright, 1928, by Robert H. Coleman.   W. F. Sherwin.
Arr. by B. B. McKinney.

1. Day is dy-ing in the west, Heav'n is touching earth with rest;
2. Lord of life, be-neath the dome Of the u-ni-verse, Thy home,
3. While the deep'ning shad-ows fall, Heart of Love, en-fold-ing all,
4. When for-ev-er from our sight Pass the stars, the day, the night,

Wait and wor-ship while the night Sets her ev-'ning lamps a-light
Gath-er us, who seek   Thy face, To the fold of Thy embrace,
Thro' the glo-ry and   the grace Of the stars that veil Thy face,
Lord of an-gels, on   our eyes Let e-ter-nal morn-ing rise,

REFRAIN.

Thro' all the sky,
For Thou art nigh.   Ho-ly, ho-ly, ho-ly,
Our hearts as-cend.
And shad-ows end.

Lord God of Hosts! Heav'n and earth are full of Thee!

Heav'n and earth are prais-ing Thee, O Lord most high!

No. 38 I Want My Life To Tell.

Mrs. Frank A. Breck. E. S. Lorenz.

1. A-mid life's bus-y, hurrying throng, The gay, the sad, the weak, the strong,
2. I want to be a bea-con light, To cheer way-far-ers in their night,
3. I want my life with Je-sus hid, That I may do what He shall bid;
4. To wealth and fame I would not climb, But I would know God's peace sublime;

While I am trav-el-ing a-long, I want my life to tell for Je-sus.
And help them on their way a-right; I want my life to tell for Je-sus.
I want to love as Je-sus did; I want my life to tell for Je-sus.
And ev-'ry-where—and all the time, I want my life to tell for Je-sus.

CHORUS.
I want my life............ to tell for Je-sus! I want my
　　　　I want my life

life............ I want my life to tell for Je-sus, That ev-'ry-where I go,

Men may His goodness know, I want my life to tell for Je-sus!

No. 39 **Somebody Here Needs Jesus.**

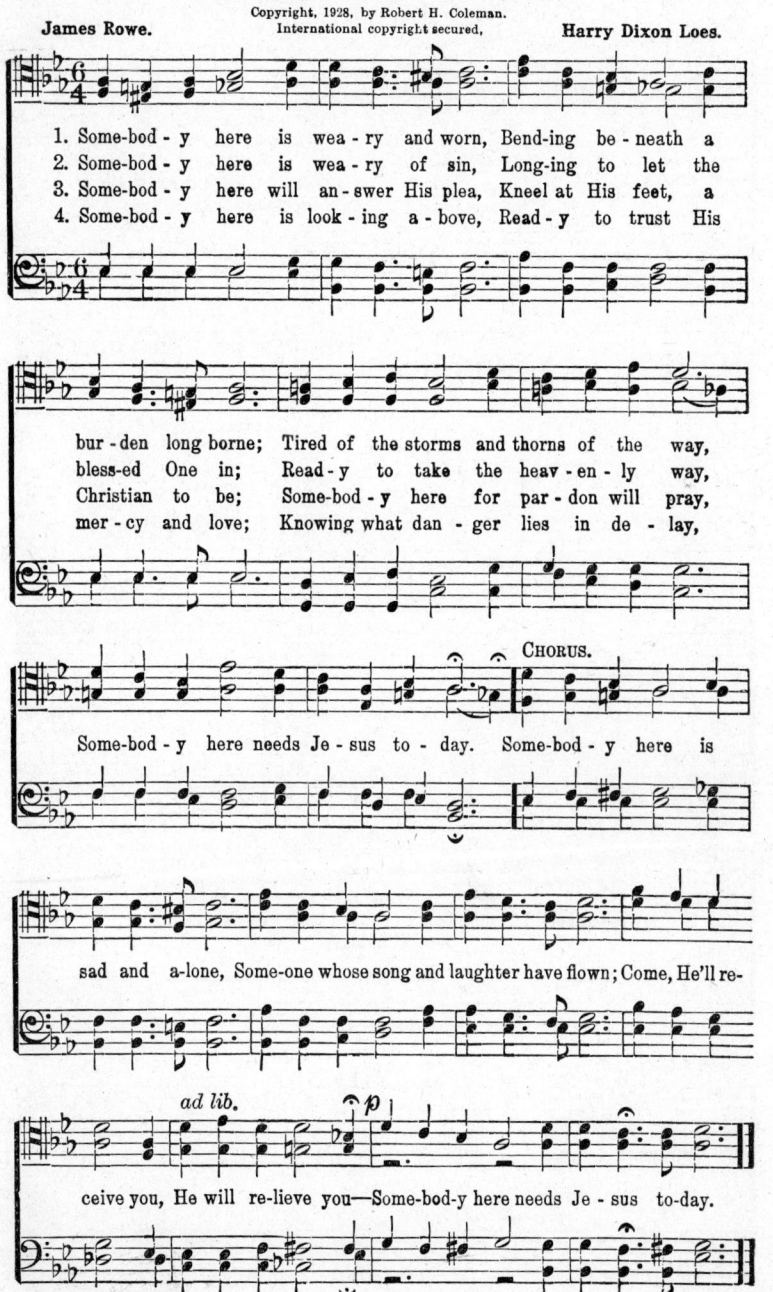

James Rowe.   Harry Dixon Loes.
Copyright, 1928, by Robert H. Coleman.
International copyright secured.

1. Some-bod-y here is wea-ry and worn, Bend-ing be-neath a bur-den long borne; Tired of the storms and thorns of the way,
2. Some-bod-y here is wea-ry of sin, Long-ing to let the bless-ed One in; Read-y to take the heav-en-ly way,
3. Some-bod-y here will an-swer His plea, Kneel at His feet, a Christian to be; Some-bod-y here for par-don will pray,
4. Some-bod-y here is look-ing a-bove, Read-y to trust His mer-cy and love; Knowing what dan-ger lies in de-lay,

CHORUS.

Some-bod-y here needs Je-sus to-day. Some-bod-y here is sad and a-lone, Some-one whose song and laughter have flown; Come, He'll re-

ad lib.

ceive you, He will re-lieve you—Some-bod-y here needs Je-sus to-day.

No. 40 My Anchor Holds Me.

H. G. T.
QUARTETTE, OR MEN IN UNISON.

Herbert G. Tovey.

1. In the Rock of a - ges I am there se - cure;
2. He will nev - er leave me, Al - ways is the same;
3. When the dark clouds gath - er, Then I feel Him near;
4. Je - sus is my ref - uge, Liv - ing Rock di - vine;

And tho' fierce the storm may rage, He, my ref - uge, will en - dure.
He will nev - er fail my soul, Ev - er - last - ing is His name.
For in Him my an - chor holds, I will nev - er, nev - er fear.
And my faith in Him a - bove Is my an - chor's liv - ing line.

CHORUS.

My an - chor holds me, My an - chor holds me,
it firm - ly holds it firm - ly holds,

Tho' the storms of sin com - bine;........ My an - chor holds me,
com - bine; it firm - ly holds,

It firm - ly holds me, For I'm anchored in the Rock di - vine......
di - vine.

No. 41 Don't Forget To Pray.

B. B. M. Copyright, 1825, by Robert H. Coleman. B. B. McKinney.

1. When the morning light is dawn-ing, Don't forget to kneel and pray;
2. While the day is swift-ly pass-ing, Keep your mind on God above;
3. When the ev'ning sun is hid-den, 'Neath the golden tint-ed west,
4. All a-long your pilgrim jour-ney, Nev-er free from sin and care;

Ask the Sav-ior to go with you, Through the burdens of the day.
Ask-ing Him to ev-er guide you, In the pathway of His love.
Al-ways pray for His pro-tec-tion, Through a night of peaceful rest.
You will o-ver-come temp-ta-tion, In the se-cret place of pray'r.

CHORUS.

Don't for-get, don't for-get, Don't for-
Don't for-get to pray, don't for-get to pray,

get to kneel and pray, Don't for-get,
kneel and pray, Don't for-get to pray,

don't for-get, Don't for-get to kneel and pray.
don't for-get to pray,

No. 42 Just Outside The Door.

James Rowe.
Copyright, 1912, by B. D. Ackley.
Homer A. Rodeheaver, owner.
B. D. Ackley.

1. Oh, wea-ry soul, the gate is near, In sin why still a-bide?
2. For-give-ness Je-sus will im-part—To save your soul He died;
3. The day of life is pass-ing by, Soon night your soul will hide;
4. Come in, be free from chains of sin, Be glad, be sat-is-fied;

Both peace and rest are wait-ing here And you are just out-side.
How can you still of-fend His heart, By stay-ing just out-side?
And then "too late" will be your cry, If you are just out-side!
Be-fore the temp-est breaks, come in, And leave your past out-side.

CHORUS.

Just out-side the door, just out-side the door, Be-hold it stands a-jar!

Just out-side the door, just out-side the door, So near and yet so far!

No. 43 Shall I Crucify Him?

Copyright, 1900, by Tullar-Meredith Co.

Mrs. Frank A. Breck.

Arr. by I. H. M.
Grant Colfax Tullar.

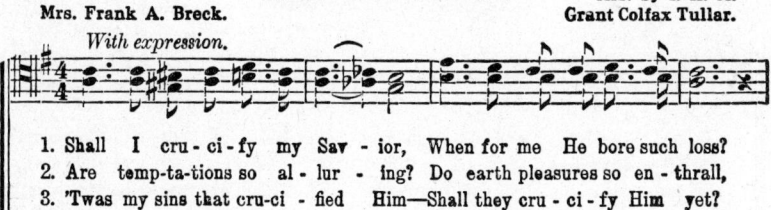

With expression.

1. Shall I cru-ci-fy my Sav-ior, When for me He bore such loss?
2. Are temp-ta-tions so al-lur-ing? Do earth pleasures so en-thrall,
3. 'Twas my sins that cru-ci-fied Him—Shall they cru-ci-fy Him yet?
4. Oh! the kind-ly hands of Je-sus, Pour-ing bless-ings on all men!

Shall I put to shame my Sav-ior? Can I nail Him to the cross?
That I can-not love my Sav-ior Well e-nough to leave them all?
Black-est day of name-less an-guish, Can my thankless soul for-get?
Bleeding, nail-scarred hands of Je-sus! Can I nail them once a-gain?

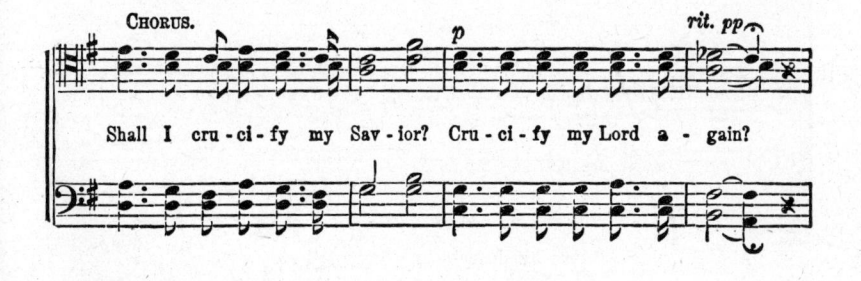

CHORUS.

Shall I cru-ci-fy my Sav-ior? Cru-ci-fy my Lord a-gain?

Once! oh once! I cru-ci-fied Him! Shall I cru-ci-fy a-gain?

No. 44. No Night There.

John R. Clements.
Moderato.

Copyright, 1927. Renewal.
Hope Publishing Co., Owner.

Hart P. Davis.
Arr. P. H. Metcalf.

1. In the land of fade-less day, Lies the cit-y four-square;
2. All the gates of pearl are made, In the cit-y four-square;
3. And the gates shall nev-er close, In the cit-y four-square;
4. There they need no sun-shine bright, In the cit-y four-square;

It shall nev-er pass a-way, And there is no night there.
All the streets with gold are laid, And there is no night there.
There life's crys-tal riv-er flows, And there is no night there.
For the Lamb is all the light, And there is no night there.

CHORUS.
mf
God shall wipe a-way all tears; There's no death, no pain, nor fears;
God shall wipe away all tears; There's no death, no pain, nor fears;
God shall wipe a-way all tears; There's no death, no pain, nor fears:

And they count not time by years, by years,
dim.
And they count not time by years, For there is no night there.
And they count not time by years, by years, For there is no night there.
For there is no night there.

No. 45 Sail On!

C. H. G.

Copyright, 1909, by Chas. H. Gabriel.
H. A. Rodeheaver, owner.

Chas. H. Gabriel.

1. Up-on a wide and stormy sea, Thou'rt sail-ing to e-ter-ni-ty,
2. Art far from shore and weary worn—The sky o'er-cast, Thy canvass torn?
3. Do comrades tremble and re-fuse To fur-ther dare the taunting hues?
4. Do snarl-ing waves thy craft assail? Art pow'r-less, drifting with the gale?

And thy great Ad-m'ral or-ders thee, "Sail on, sail on, sail on!"
Hark ye! A voice is to Thee borne, "Sail on, sail on, sail on!"
No oth-er course is thine to choose, "Sail on, sail on, sail on!"
Take heart! God's word shall nev-er fail— Sail on, sail on, sail on!"

CHORUS. *Faster.*

Sail on! sail on! the storms will soon be past, The darkness will not al-ways last! Sail on! sail on! God lives! and He commands: "Sail on! sail on!"
sail on! sail on!

No. 46   Shine On Me.

Words by
B. B. McK.   Arr. copyright, 1928, by Robert H. Coleman.   Arr. by
B. B. McKinney.

1. My ship is sail-ing o'er the sea, The unknown restless sea;
2. Thro' storm and gale I can-not see The bil-lows 'round me roll;
3. I see, I see, dear Lord, the light, It's shin-ing bright for me;
4. O sail-or, drift-ing with the tide, And tossed by wind and wave,

Oh, Je-sus, let the light-house shine Its gold-en beams on me.
Dear Je-sus, ride a-long with me, I yield to Thy con-trol.
'Twill guide me to my home a-bove, And thro' e-ter-ni-ty.
Oh, look to Je-sus Christ for light, And He'll com-plete-ly save.

CHORUS. *Arr.*

Shine on me, shine on me, Let the light from the lighthouse shine on me;

Oh, shine on me, shine on me, Let the light from the lighthouse shine on me.

No. 47   Jesus, The Light of the World.

Arr. copyright, 1921, by Rob't H. Coleman.

J. V. C.   Arranged I. E. R.

1. All ye saints of light pro-claim, Je-sus, the Light of the world;
2. Hear the Sav-ior's ear-nest call, Je-sus, the Light of the world;
3. Why not seek Him then to-day, Je-sus, the Light of the world;
4. Come, con-fess Him as your King, Je-sus, the Light of the world;

Life and mer-cy in His name, Je-sus, the Light of the world.
Send the gos-pel truth to all, Je-sus, the Light of the world.
Go with truth the nar-row way, Je-sus, the Light of the world.
Then the bells of heav'n will ring, Je-sus, the Light of the world.

CHORUS.

We'll walk in the light, beau-ti-ful light, Come where the dewdrops of mercy are bright;

Shine all a-round us by day and by night, Je-sus, the Light of the world.

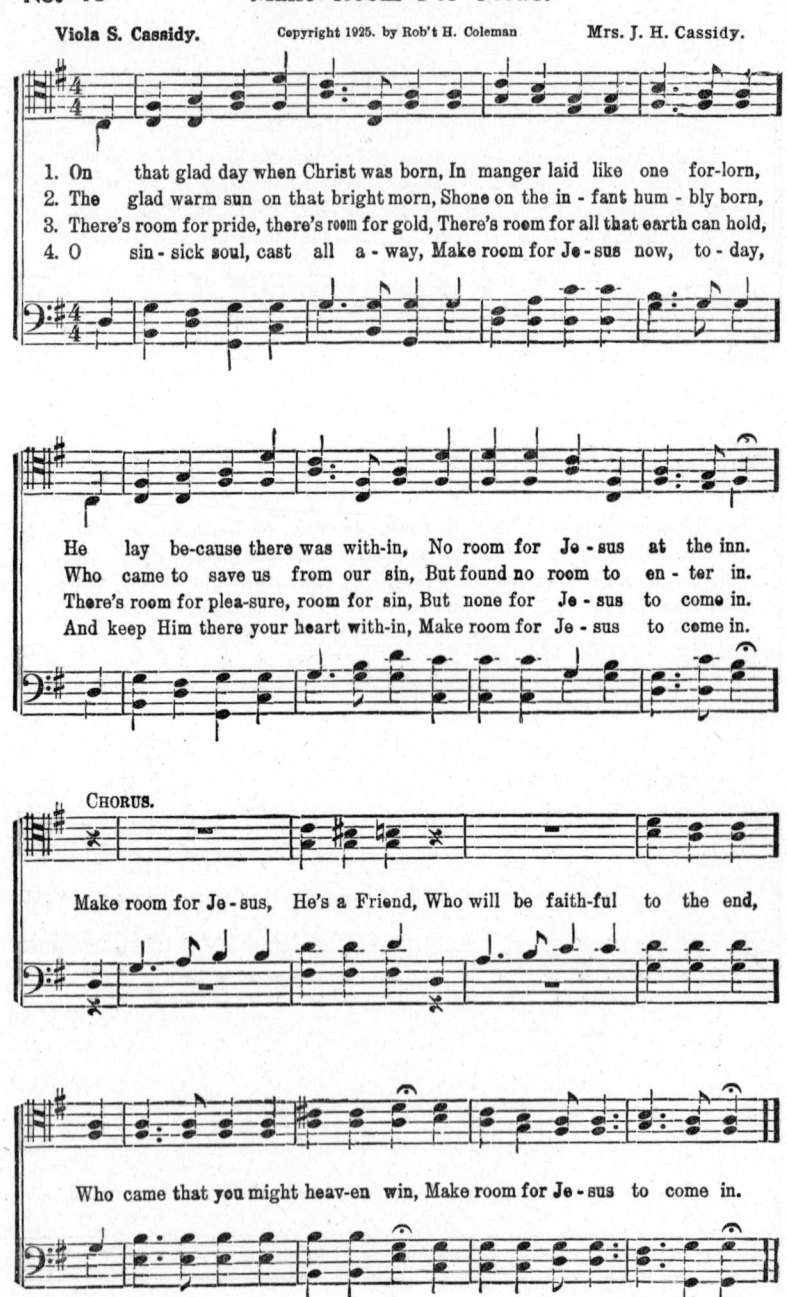

No. 48   **Make Room For Jesus.**

Viola S. Cassidy.   Copyright 1925. by Rob't H. Coleman   Mrs. J. H. Cassidy.

1. On that glad day when Christ was born, In manger laid like one for-lorn,
2. The glad warm sun on that bright morn, Shone on the in-fant hum-bly born,
3. There's room for pride, there's room for gold, There's room for all that earth can hold,
4. O sin-sick soul, cast all a-way, Make room for Je-sus now, to-day,

He lay be-cause there was with-in, No room for Je-sus at the inn.
Who came to save us from our sin, But found no room to en-ter in.
There's room for plea-sure, room for sin, But none for Je-sus to come in.
And keep Him there your heart with-in, Make room for Je-sus to come in.

CHORUS.

Make room for Je-sus, He's a Friend, Who will be faith-ful to the end,

Who came that you might heav-en win, Make room for Je-sus to come in.

No. 49   I Am Safe.

Copyright 1916, by Rob't H. Coleman, Dallas, Texas.

I. E. R.   I. E. Reynolds.

1. I am safe from ev-'ry storm, Christ doth love me so;
2. I am safe when troub-les come, With my Sav-ior near;
3. I am safe for ev-er-more, Thro' the crim-son flood;
4. I am safe what-e'er be-fall, With a Friend so strong;

I am safe from ev-'ry harm, For my Lord I know.
I am safe from Sa-tan's wiles, For my pray'r He'll hear.
I am safe and Christ I'll see, By His pre-cious blood.
I am safe for heav'n and home, With the blood-washed throng.

Chorus.

I am safe, I am safe, For my Sav-ior died for me;
So safe, so safe,

I am safe, so safe, I am safe in Him, In His likeness I shall be.
shall be.

No. 50 Going Home.

William Hunter Copyright, 1932, by Robert H. Coleman. B. B. McKinney.

1. My heav'nly home is bright and fair; Nor pain, nor death can en-ter there;
2. My Father's house is built on high, Far, far a-bove the star-ry sky;
3. While here a stranger far from home, Af-flic-tion's waves may round me foam;
4. Let oth-ers seek a home be-low, Which flames devour or waves o'erflow;

Its glitt'ring tow'rs the sun out-shine; That heav'nly mansion shall be mine.
When from this earthly pris-on free, That heav'nly mansion mine shall be.
Al-tho', like Lazarus, sick and poor, My heav'nly mansion is se-cure.
Be mine the happier lot to own A heav'nly mansion near the throne.

CHORUS.

Home, ... Home, ... I am go-ing home,
I am going home, I am go-ing home,

Home, ... Home, ... I am go-ing home.
I am go-ing home, I am go-ing home,

No. 51   The Church In The Wildwood.

W. S. P.   Dr. Wm. S. Pitts.

1. There's a church in the val-ley by the wild-wood, No lov-li-er place in the dale; No spot is so dear to my child-hood As the lit-tle brown church in the vale.
2. How sweet on a clear Sab-bath morn-ing To list to the clear ringing bell; Its tones so sweet-ly are call-ing, Oh, come to the church in the vale.
3. There, close by the church in the val-ley, Lies one that I loved so well; She sleeps, sweetly sleeps 'neath the wil-low, Dis-turb not her rest in the vale.
4. There, close by the side of that loved one, 'Neath the tree where the wild flow-ers bloom, When the fare-well hymn shall be chant-ed, I shall rest by her side in the tomb.

D. S.—spot is so dear to my child-hood As the lit-tle brown church in the vale.

FINE.   CHORUS.

Oh, come, come, come, come, come, come, church by the wild-wood, Oh, come to the church in the dale; No come, come, come, come, come, come, come, come, come, come, come, come,

No. 52   The Haven Of Rest.

Arr. copyright, 1928, by Robert H. Coleman.

H. L. Gilmour. Geo. D. Moore.
Arr. by B. B. McKinney.

1. My soul in sad ex-ile was out on life's sea, So burdened with
2. I yield-ed my-self to His ten-der em-brace, And faith tak-ing
3. The song of my soul, since the Lord made me whole, Has been the old
4. How pre-cious the thought that we all may re-cline, Like John the be-
5. Oh, come to the Sav-iour, He pa-tient-ly waits To save by His

sin and dis-trest, Till I heard a sweet voice say-ing, "Make Me your
hold of the Word, My fet-ters fell off, and I anchored my
sto-ry so blest, Of Jesus, who'll save who-so-ev-er will
lov-ed and blest, On Jesus' strong arm, where no tempest can
pow-er di-vine; Come, an-chor your soul in the "Ha-ven of

D. S.—The tempest may sweep o'er the wild, stormy

FINE. CHORUS.

choice;" And I entered the "Ha-ven of Rest!"
soul; The "Ha-ven of Rest" is my Lord.
have A home in the "Ha-ven of Rest!"   I've anchored my
harm,— Se-cure in the "Ha-ven of Rest!"
Rest," And say, "My Be-lov-ed is mine."

deep, In Je-sus I'm safe ev-er-more.

soul in the "Ha-ven of Rest," I'll sail the wide seas no more;

No. 53 The Ninety And Nine

As arranged for and sung by the Bel-Canto Quartet, Dallas, Texas.

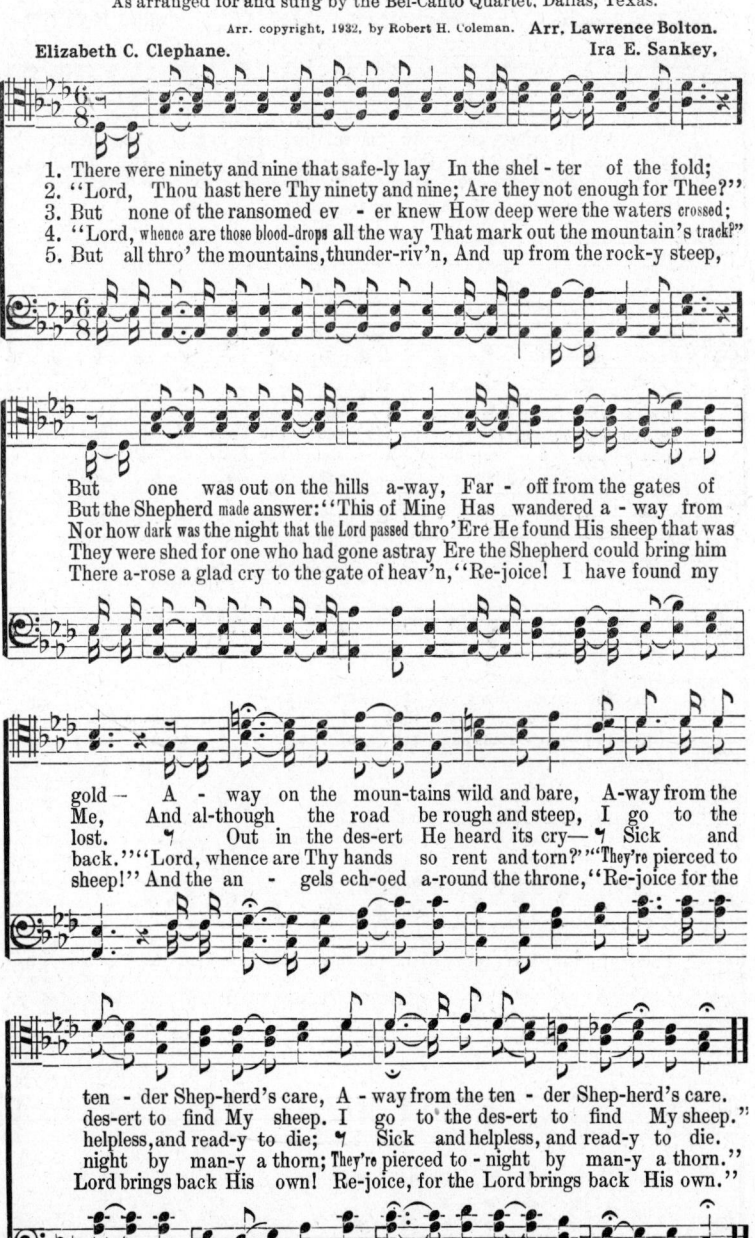

Arr. copyright, 1932, by Robert H. Coleman. **Arr. Lawrence Bolton.**

Elizabeth C. Clephane.   Ira E. Sankey.

1. There were ninety and nine that safe-ly lay In the shel - ter of the fold;
2. "Lord, Thou hast here Thy ninety and nine; Are they not enough for Thee?"
3. But none of the ransomed ev - er knew How deep were the waters crossed;
4. "Lord, whence are those blood-drops all the way That mark out the mountain's track?"
5. But all thro' the mountains, thunder-riv'n, And up from the rock-y steep,

But one was out on the hills a-way, Far - off from the gates of
But the Shepherd made answer: "This of Mine Has wandered a - way from
Nor how dark was the night that the Lord passed thro' Ere He found His sheep that was
They were shed for one who had gone astray Ere the Shepherd could bring him
There a-rose a glad cry to the gate of heav'n, "Re-joice! I have found my

gold — A - way on the moun-tains wild and bare, A-way from the
Me, And al-though the road be rough and steep, I go to the
lost. Out in the des-ert He heard its cry— Sick and
back." "Lord, whence are Thy hands so rent and torn?" "They're pierced to
sheep!" And the an - gels ech-oed a-round the throne, "Re-joice for the

ten - der Shep-herd's care, A - way from the ten - der Shep-herd's care.
des-ert to find My sheep. I go to the des-ert to find My sheep."
helpless, and read-y to die; Sick and helpless, and read-y to die.
night by man-y a thorn; They're pierced to - night by man-y a thorn."
Lord brings back His own! Re-joice, for the Lord brings back His own."

No. 54 The Face Of The Master.

Copyright, 1928, by Robert H. Coleman.
International copyright secured

Mrs. R. W. Leader.
Mrs. J. H. Cassidy.

SOLO.

1. In the ear-ly morn, in my gar-den, Where flow'rs waft per-fume rare; I see the Face of the Mas-ter, In the rose He gives to me there.
2. In the noon-time's hur-ry and wor-ry, In the crowds that throng the street; I see the Face of the Mas-ter, In the glance of souls that I meet.
3. In the eve when work is all o-ver, More beau-ties I be-hold; I see the Face of the Mas-ter, In the glo-rious sun-set of gold.

CHORUS.

O how dear, the Face of the Mas-ter, And to me how pre-cious His touch; I yield a-new to the Sav-iour, Whose love has meant so much.

No. 55 An Eye That Never Sleeps.

As arranged for and sung by the Bel-Canto Quartet, Dallas, Texas.

John A. Wallace. Arr. copyright, 1932, by Robert H. Coleman. Arr. Lawrence Bolton.

1. There is an eye that nev-er sleeps Be-neath the wing of night;
2. There is an arm that nev-er tires When hu-man strength gives way;
3. But there's a pow'r which man can wield, When mor-tal aid is vain,

There is an ear that nev-er shuts, When sink the beams of light.
There is a love that nev-er fails When earth-ly loves de-cay.
That eye, that arm, that love to reach, That lis-t'ning ear to gain.

No. 56 Holy Bible, Book Divine.

As arranged for and sung by the Bel-Canto Quartet, Dallas, Texas.

Arr by Lawrence Bolton.

John Burton. Arr. copyright, 1932, by Robert H. Coleman, Wm. B. Bradbury.

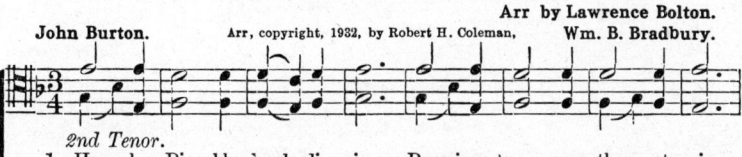

1. Ho-ly Bi-ble, book di-vine, Pre-cious treas-ure, thou art mine;
2. Mine to chide me when I rove; Mine to show a Sav-iour's love;
3. Mine to com-fort in dis-tress, Suf-f'ring in this wil-der-ness;

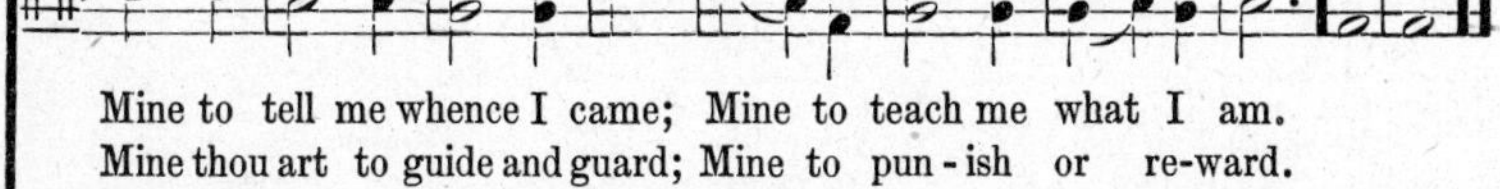

Mine to tell me whence I came; Mine to teach me what I am.
Mine thou art to guide and guard; Mine to pun-ish or re-ward.
Mine to show by liv-ing faith, Man can tri-umph o-ver death. A-men.

No. 57   The Just Shall Walk By Faith.

W. E. B. Lockridge.   Copyright, 1932, by Robert H. Coleman.   **John D. Hammond.**

1. There is a land of one great light, The home of God and grace and love;
2. The land's great light is God's dear Son, Who saves His own by His shed blood;
3. They fear no more the heat of sun, They rest se-cure in His great might;

And bright it is to those a-bove, It is the home of good and right.
They plunged beneath the sacred flood, His heart and theirs is made but one.
And lay them down in peace at night, Now that the worldly task is done.

CHORUS.

The just shall walk by faith, His life shall be a march of trust;

Thru His love we are called the just, The just shall walk by faith.

No. 58   Come, Ye Disconsolate.

As arranged for and sung by the Bel-Canto Quartet, Dallas, Texas.

Arr. by Lawrence Bolton.
Thomas Moore.   Arr. copyright, 1932, by Robert H Coleman.   **Samuel Webbe.**

1. Come, ye dis-con-so-late, wher-e'er you lan-guish; Come to the
2. Joy of the des-o-late, light of the stray-ing, Hope of the
3. Here see the bread of life; see wa-ters flow-ing Forth from the

Baritone.

Come, Ye Disconsolate. Concluded.

2nd Tenor.

mer - cy-seat, fer - vent - ly kneel; Here bring your wounded hearts,
pen - i - tent, fade - less and pure, Here speaks the Com-fort-er,
throne of God, pure from a - bove; Come to the feast of love;

here tell your an-guish; Earth has no sor-row that Heav'n cannot heal.
ten - der - ly say-ing, "Earth has no sor-row that Heav'n cannot cure."
come, ev - er know - ing Earth has no sor-row but Heav'n can re-move.

No. 59 Come Unto Me, Ye Weary.

As arranged for and sung by the Bel-Canto Quartet, Dallas, Texas.

W. C. Dix.   Arr. copyright, 1932, by Robert H. Coleman.   Arr. Lawrence Bolton.

1st Tenor.   **2nd Tenor.**

1. "Come un - to Me, ye wea - ry, And I will give you rest." Oh, bless-ed
2. "Come un - to Me, ye faint-ing, And I will give you life." Oh, peaceful
3. "And who-so-ev - er com - eth I will not cast him out." Oh, pa-tient

voice of Je-sus, Which comes to hearts opprest; It tells of ben - e - dic-tion, Of
voice of Je-sus Which comes to end our strife; The foe is stern and ea - ger, The
love of Je-sus, Which drives away our doubt; Which calls us - ver-y sin-ners, Un-

2nd Baritone.   *1st Tenor.*

pardon, grace and peace, Of joy that hath no end-ing, Of love which cannot cease.
fight is fierce and long; But Thou hast made me mighty, And stronger than the strong.
worth-y tho' we be Of love so free and boundless,—To come, dear Lord, to Thee.

No. 60   My Anchor Holds.

Copyright 1930, Renewal. Hope Publishing Co., Owner.
Used by Permission.

W. C. Martin.   D. B. Towner.

1. Tho' the an-gry sur-ges roll On my tem-pest-driv-en soul;
2. Might-y tides a-bout me sweep, Per-ils lurk with-in the deep;
3. Troub-les al-most whelm the soul; Griefs like bil-lows o'er me roll;

I am peace-ful, for I know, Wild-ly tho' the winds may blow,
An-gry clouds o'ershade the sky, And the tem-pest ri-ses high;
Temp-ters seek to lure a-stray, Storms ob-scure the light of day:

I've an an-chor safe and sure, And in Christ I shall en-dure.
Still I stand the tem-pest's shock, For my an-chor grips the rock.
But in Christ I can be bold,—I've an an-chor that shall hold.

CHORUS.

And it holds, my an-chor holds;   Blow your wild-est, then, ye
And it holds,..... my an-chor holds; Blow your wild - est

gale, On my bark so small and frail; I shall nev-er, nev-er

My Anchor Holds.

fail, For my an - chor holds, my an - chor holds.
For my an - chor holds, it firm - ly holds,

No. 61   **There's No Friend Like Jesus.**

Copyright, 1917, by Robert H. Coleman.

M. J. B.   M. J. Babbitt.
                                                                                    Arr. I. E. R.

1. There's no friend to me like Je - sus, He my ev - 'ry need sup - plies;
2. All, yes, all to me is Je - sus, Blest Re - deem - er, Saviour, Guide;
3. I will nev - er cease to love Him, He who died to set me free;

He not on - ly saves but keeps me, Noth-ing good from me de - nies.
And from ev - 'ry foe de - fends me, And in Him I'll ev - er hide.
Now in Him I am a - bid - ing, And some day His face I'll see.

Chorus.

Yes, in Him I'm ful - ly trust - ing, Yes, thro' Him I'll con - quer all;

For I know He saves and keeps me, And He'll nev - er let me fall.

No. 62. The Wayside Cross.

Copyright, 1884, by H. R. Palmer.

C. L. St. John.   Used by permission.   H. R. Palmer.

Solo, *ad lib.* (*Declamatory style.*)

1. "Which way shall I take," shouts a voice on the night, "I'm a pilgrim a-wearied, and spent is my light; And I seek for a pal-ace, that rests on the hill, But between us, a stream li-eth sul-len and chill."
2. "Which way shall I take for the bright golden span That bridg-es the wa-ters so safe-ly for man? To the right? to the left? ah, me! if I knew—The night is so dark, and the pass-ers so few."
4. "See the lights from the palace in sil-ver-y lines, How they pencil the hedg-es and fruit-la-den vines—My fortune! my all! for one tan-gled gleam That sifts thro' the lil-ies, and wastes on the stream."

Slower, and sustained.

Chorus.

Near, near thee, my son, is the old way-side cross, Like a gray fri-ar cowled in li-chens and moss: And its crossbeam will point to the bright golden span That

*The chorus should begin while the solo voice is still holding the last note.

The Wayside Cross.

CODA. *pp To be sung after last stanza.*

bridges the waters so safely for man, That bridges the waters so safely for man.

No. 63
What Did He Do?

Copyright 1931, Renewal.
Hope Publishing Co., Owner.
Used by Permission.

Dr. J. M. Gray.
W. Owen.
Arr. by O. F. Pugh.

1. O lis-ten to our wondrous sto-ry: Counted once a-mong the lost,
2. No an-gel could His place have tak-en, Highest of the high tho' He:
3. Will you sur-ren-der to this Sav-ior? To His scep-ter hum-bly bow?

Yet, One came down from heaven's glo-ry, Saving us at aw-ful cost!
The loved One on the cross for-sak-en Was one of the God-head Three!
You, too, shall come to know His fa-vor; He will save you, save you now.

CHORUS.

Who saved us from e-ter-nal loss? What did He do?
Who but God's Son up-on the cross? He

Where is He now? In heav-en in-ter-ced-ing!
died for you! Be-lieve it thou, In

No. 64 The Old Road.

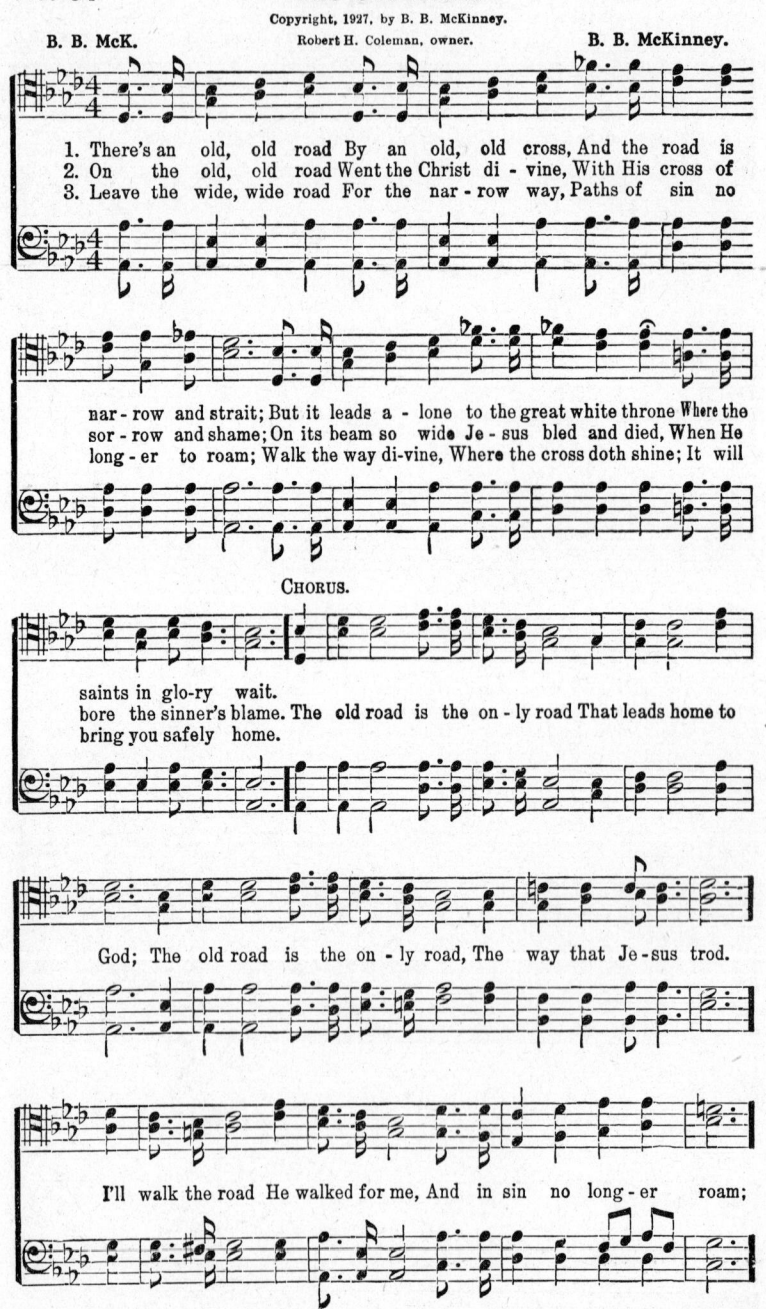

Copyright, 1927, by B. B. McKinney.
Robert H. Coleman, owner.

B. B. McK.   B. B. McKinney.

1. There's an old, old road By an old, old cross, And the road is nar-row and strait; But it leads a-lone to the great white throne Where the saints in glo-ry wait.
2. On the old, old road Went the Christ di-vine, With His cross of sor-row and shame; On its beam so wide Je-sus bled and died, When He bore the sinner's blame.
3. Leave the wide, wide road For the nar-row way, Paths of sin no long-er to roam; Walk the way di-vine, Where the cross doth shine; It will bring you safely home.

CHORUS.

The old road is the on-ly road That leads home to God; The old road is the on-ly road, The way that Je-sus trod. I'll walk the road He walked for me, And in sin no long-er roam;

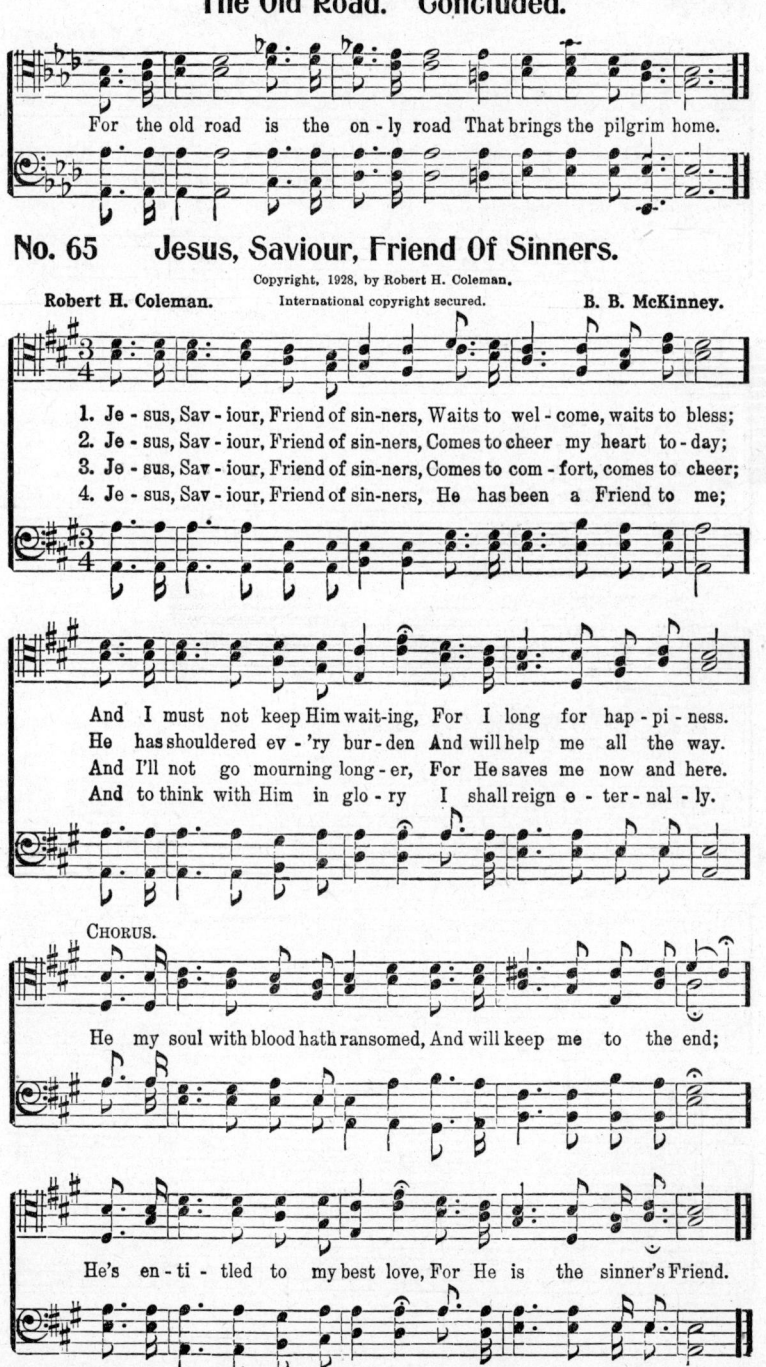

The Old Road. Concluded.

For the old road is the on-ly road That brings the pilgrim home.

No. 65   Jesus, Saviour, Friend Of Sinners.

Copyright, 1928, by Robert H. Coleman.
International copyright secured.

Robert H. Coleman.   B. B. McKinney.

1. Je-sus, Sav-iour, Friend of sin-ners, Waits to wel-come, waits to bless;
2. Je-sus, Sav-iour, Friend of sin-ners, Comes to cheer my heart to-day;
3. Je-sus, Sav-iour, Friend of sin-ners, Comes to com-fort, comes to cheer;
4. Je-sus, Sav-iour, Friend of sin-ners, He has been a Friend to me;

And I must not keep Him wait-ing, For I long for hap-pi-ness.
He has shouldered ev-'ry bur-den And will help me all the way.
And I'll not go mourning long-er, For He saves me now and here.
And to think with Him in glo-ry I shall reign e-ter-nal-ly.

CHORUS.

He my soul with blood hath ransomed, And will keep me to the end;

He's en-ti-tled to my best love, For He is the sinner's Friend.

SM-3

No. 66 **Going Down The Valley.**

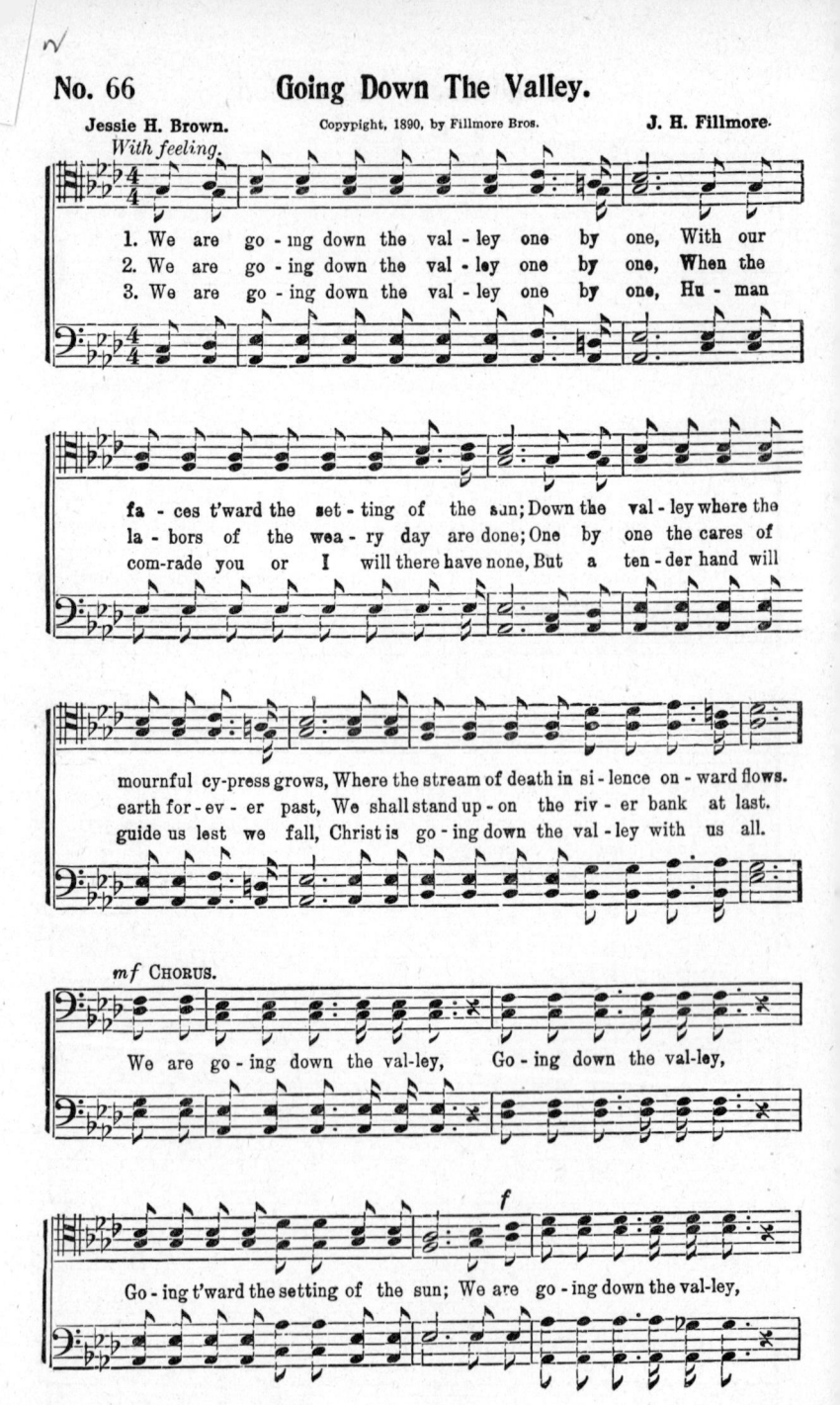

Jessie H. Brown. Copyright, 1890, by Fillmore Bros. J. H. Fillmore.

With feeling.

1. We are go-ing down the val-ley one by one, With our fa-ces t'ward the set-ting of the sun; Down the val-ley where the mournful cy-press grows, Where the stream of death in si-lence on-ward flows.
2. We are go-ing down the val-ley one by one, When the la-bors of the wea-ry day are done; One by one the cares of earth for-ev-er past, We shall stand up-on the riv-er bank at last.
3. We are go-ing down the val-ley one by one, Hu-man com-rade you or I will there have none, But a ten-der hand will guide us lest we fall, Christ is go-ing down the val-ley with us all.

mf CHORUS.

We are go-ing down the val-ley, Go-ing down the val-ley,

f

Go-ing t'ward the setting of the sun; We are go-ing down the val-ley,

Going Down The Valley.

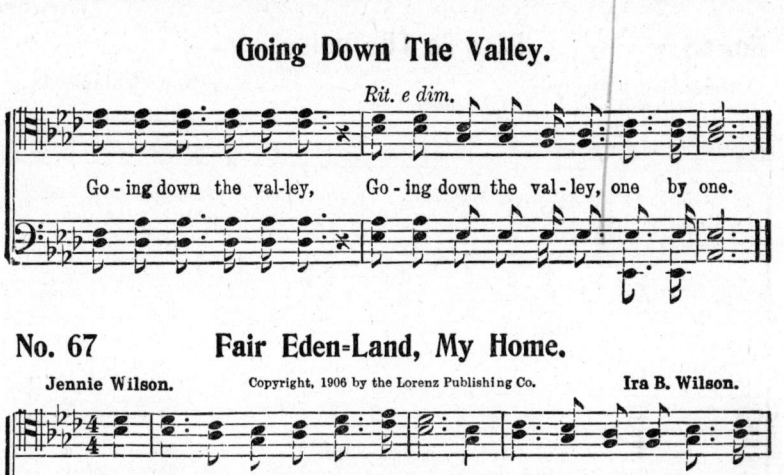

Rit. e dim.

Go-ing down the val-ley, Go-ing down the val-ley, one by one.

No. 67 Fair Eden=Land, My Home.

Jennie Wilson.   Copyright, 1906 by the Lorenz Publishing Co.   Ira B. Wilson.

1. By faith I see thy hap-py shore, Where earthly tri-als come no more; There I shall rest with conflicts o'er, Fair E-den-land, my home.
2. Made pure from ev-'ry taint of wrong, I long to sing redemption's song A-mong thy ho-ly ransomed throng, Fair E-den-land, my home.
3. In thy do-main I shall be-hold E-ter-nal mys-ter-ies un-fold, And see my Lord with joy un-told, Fair E-den-land, my home.

CHORUS.

Fair E-den-land, my home! Fair E-den-land, my home! I long to stand up-on Thy strand, Fair E-den-land, my home, (my home.)

No. 68 List To The Voice.

Arr. copyright, 1924, by Robert H. Coleman.

Words by B. B. McKinney.　　　　Arr. by B. B. McKinney.
Duet for Tenor and Baritone.

1. List to the voice of the Sav-iour Com-ing from heav-en a-bove,... Filled with a mes-sage so ten-der, Filled with a mes-sage of love;.... Soft-ly it speaks to the wea-ry, Ten-der-ly speaks to the sad,..... Turn-ing their night in-to morn-ing, Mak-ing the lone-ly heart glad........

2. List to the voice of the Sav-iour Call-ing the wea-ry, op-prest,... Lov-ing-ly, ten-der-ly plead-ing, "Come, and I will give you rest."... Come with your grief and your sor-row, Come with your bur-den of sin;..... Trust in the bless-ed Re-deem-er, Life ev-er-last-ing you'll win.........

3. List to the voice of the Sav-iour Call-ing to you and to me,..... Call-ing us o-ver the tu-mult, Call-ing us o-ver the sea;..... Go, for the lost ones are stray-ing, Far from the Sav-iour they roam:.... "Go in the by-ways and hedg-es," Bring-ing the wan-der-ers home........

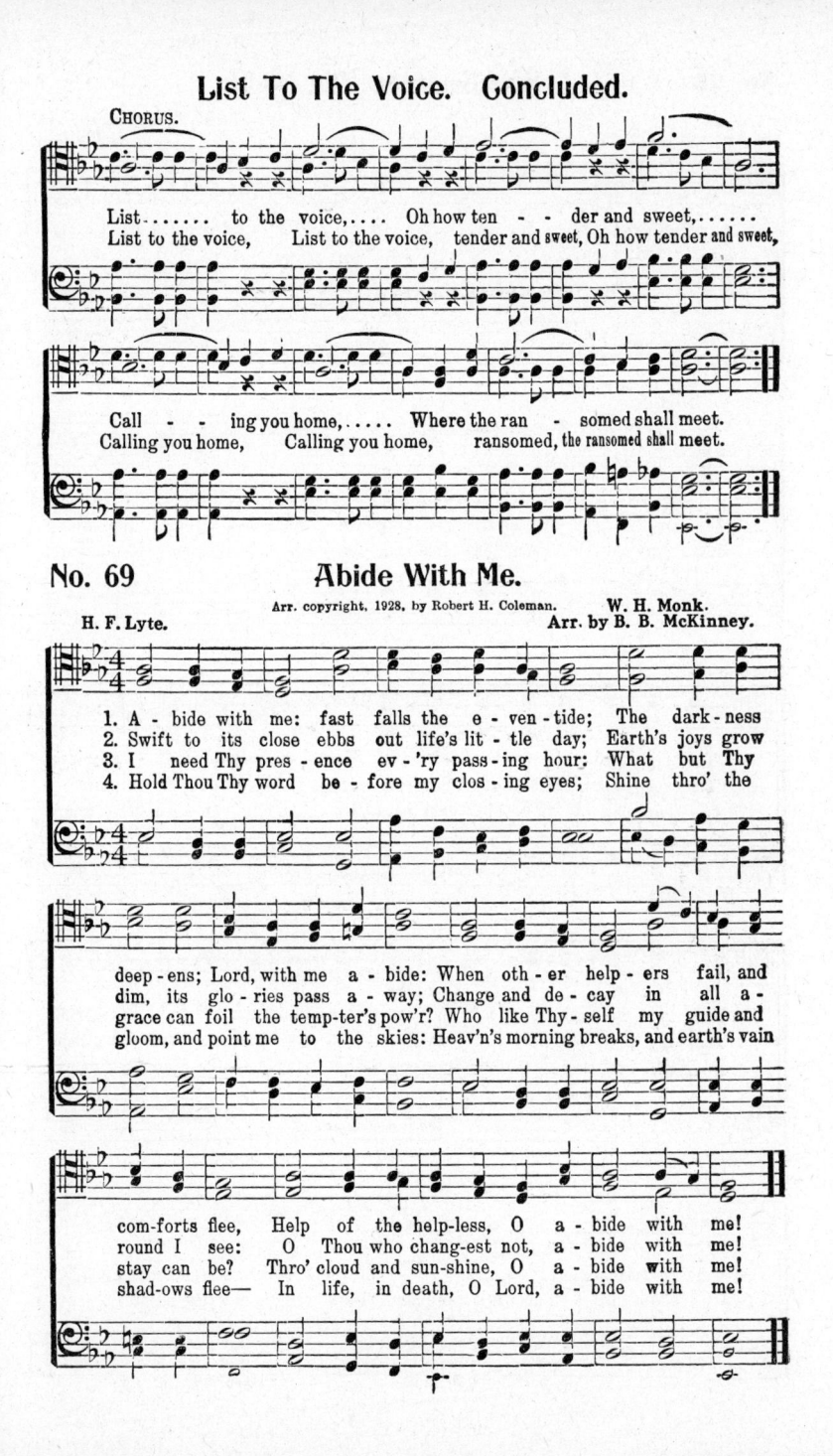

List To The Voice. Concluded.

CHORUS.

List........ to the voice,.... Oh how ten - - der and sweet,......
List to the voice, List to the voice, tender and sweet, Oh how tender and sweet,

Call - - ing you home,..... Where the ran - somed shall meet.
Calling you home, Calling you home, ransomed, the ransomed shall meet.

No. 69   Abide With Me.

H. F. Lyte.

Arr. copyright, 1928, by Robert H. Coleman.

W. H. Monk.
Arr. by B. B. McKinney.

1. A - bide with me: fast falls the e - ven - tide; The dark - ness
2. Swift to its close ebbs out life's lit - tle day; Earth's joys grow
3. I need Thy pres - ence ev - 'ry pass - ing hour: What but Thy
4. Hold Thou Thy word be - fore my clos - ing eyes; Shine thro' the

deep - ens; Lord, with me a - bide: When oth - er help - ers fail, and
dim, its glo - ries pass a - way; Change and de - cay in all a -
grace can foil the temp-ter's pow'r? Who like Thy - self my guide and
gloom, and point me to the skies: Heav'n's morning breaks, and earth's vain

com - forts flee, Help of the help-less, O a - bide with me!
round I see: O Thou who chang-est not, a - bide with me!
stay can be? Thro' cloud and sun - shine, O a - bide with me!
shad - ows flee— In life, in death, O Lord, a - bide with me!

No. 70 A Watchman In The Night.

Copyright, 1913, by M. J. Babbitt.

Julia H. Johnston.   Robert H. Coleman, owner   J. Babbitt.

1. Where the night of sin lies dark-ly, And a-far the wand'rers roam,
2. It is night up-on the wa-ter Where life's bil-lows toss and roar,
3. Not my own, the word of warn-ing Or the light of help and cheer,

I must keep the watch-fires burn-ing That will guide the wea-ry home;
I must keep my watch-fires gleaming On the sands up-on the shore;
But to me has been en-trust-ed Je-sus' mes-sage, sweet and clear;

'Tis my Lord who loves the sin-sick That has made this du-ty mine;
'Tis for this that Christ my Sav-ior Hath in love de-liv-ered me,
I can call to those in dark-ness Or far out up-on the foam;

He has giv-en to my keep-ing This fair gleam of light di-vine.
That my light may help an-oth-er Who is out up-on the sea.
I can keep my own light burn-ing That may guide the wan-d'rer home.

CHORUS.

I'm a watch-man.......... in the night. I'm a
I'm a watch-man in the night,

A Watchman In The Night.

keeper........ of a light; For the wanderer's returning I must
I'm the keeper of a light;
keep the watchfire burn-ing, I'm a watchman, I'm a watchman in the night.

No. 71   Remember Me, O Mighty One.

Anon.   Joanna Kinkel.

1 When storms around are sweeping, When lone my watch I'm keep-ing,
2. When walk-ing on life's o-cean, Con-trol its rag-ing mo-tion;
3. When weight of sin op-press-es, When dark des-pair dis-tress-es.

'Mid fires of e-vil fall-ing, 'Mid temp-ters' voi-ces call-ing,
When from its dan-gers shrink-ing, When in its dread deeps sink-ing,
All thro' the life that's mor-tal, And when I pass death's por-tal,

CHORUS.

Re-mem-ber me, O might-y One! Re-mem-ber me, O might-y One!

No. 72 **That Beautiful Land.**

May be sung as Duet by first and second tenors.

F. A. F. White.   Mark M. Jones.

1. I have heard of a land On a far a-way strand, In the Bi-ble the sto-ry is told,...... Where cares nev-er come, Nev-er dark-ness nor gloom, And noth-ing shall ev-er grow old.
2. There are ev-er-green trees That bend low in the breeze, And their fruit-age is bright-er than gold;...... There are harps for our hands, In that fair-est of lands, And noth-ing shall ev-er grow old.
3. There's a home in that land, At the Fa-ther's right hand; There are man-sions whose joys are un-told,...... And per-en-ni-al spring, Where the birds ev-er sing, And noth-ing can ev-er grow old.

CHORUS.

In that beau-ti-ful land, On that far a-way strand, No storms with their

That Beautiful Land.

blasts ev-er frown; The streets, I am told, Are paved with pure gold, And the sun shall nev-er go down.

No. 73 Let The Lower Lights Be Burning.

P. P. B.   P. P. Bliss.

1. Bright-ly beams our Fa-ther's mer-cy From His light-house ev-er-more,
2. Dark the night of sin has set-tled, Loud the an-gry bil-lows roar;
3. Trim your fee-ble lamp, my broth-er; Some poor sail-or, tem-pest-tossed,

FINE.

But to us He gives the keep-ing Of the lights a-long the shore.
Ea-ger eyes are watch-ing, long-ing, For the lights a-long the shore.
Try-ing now to make the har-bor, In the dark-ness may be lost.

D. S. Some poor fainting, struggling sea-man You may res-cue you may save.

CHORUS.   D.S.

Let the low-er lights be burn-ing, Send a gleam a-cross the wave!

No. 74. Fight To Win.

James Rowe.   Copyright 1908, by the Lorenz Pub. Co.   E. L. Ashford.

1. Sol - diers on the bat - tle field, Fight to win;
2. Tho' the strife be long and hard, Fight to win;
3. Fol - low where your Leader leads, Fight to win;

Fight to win; Fight to win.
Fight to win. Have no thought that you will yield,
Fight to win. Cour - age is its own re - ward,
Fight to win. Crown your lives with no - ble deeds,

win.   Sol - diers,
Sol-diers ev - er fight to win.

fight,   Yes, fight to win.   Man-ful - ly your col - ors
God is with you, He will
Would you thin the ranks of

Sol - diers, fight to win;   Sol - diers, fight to win;

show,   Keep your fa - ces to the foe,..............
shield,   Give your strength the sword to wield;............
wrong,   Sing at last the vic - tor's song,............

Give with cour - age blow for blow, Soldiers, fight, yes, fight to win.
Yours at last shall be the field; Soldiers, fight, yes, fight to win.
Let your faith in God be strong; Soldiers, fight, yes, fight to win.

Fight To Win.

REFRAIN. (*Time strongly marked.*)

Fight to win, yes, fight to win, Nev-er yield an inch to sin;

cres.

Keep up the fight both day and night; Sol-diers, fight, fight to win.

No. 75　　　Twilight Is Falling.

A. S. Kieffer.　　Arr. copyright 1921, by Rob't H. Coleman.　　B. C. Unseld.
　　　　　　　　　　　　　　　　　　　　　　　　　　Arr. I. E. R.

1. Twilight is fall-ing o - ver the sea, Shadows are stealing dark on the lea;
2. Voices of loved ones, songs of the past, Still linger round me while life shall last;
3. Come in the twilight, come, come to me! Bringing some message o-ver the sea,

FINE.

Borne on the night-winds, voi-ces of yore Come from the far - off shore.
Lone - ly I wan - der, sad - ly I roam, Seek - ing that far - off home.
Cheer - ing my path - way while here I roam, Seek - ing that far - off home.

D. S.—Gleameth a man - sion, filled with delight, Sweet hap - py home so bright!

CHORUS. *f*　　　　　　　　　　　　　　　　　　　　　*D. S.*

Far a-way beyond the starlit skies, Where the love-light never, nev - er dies,

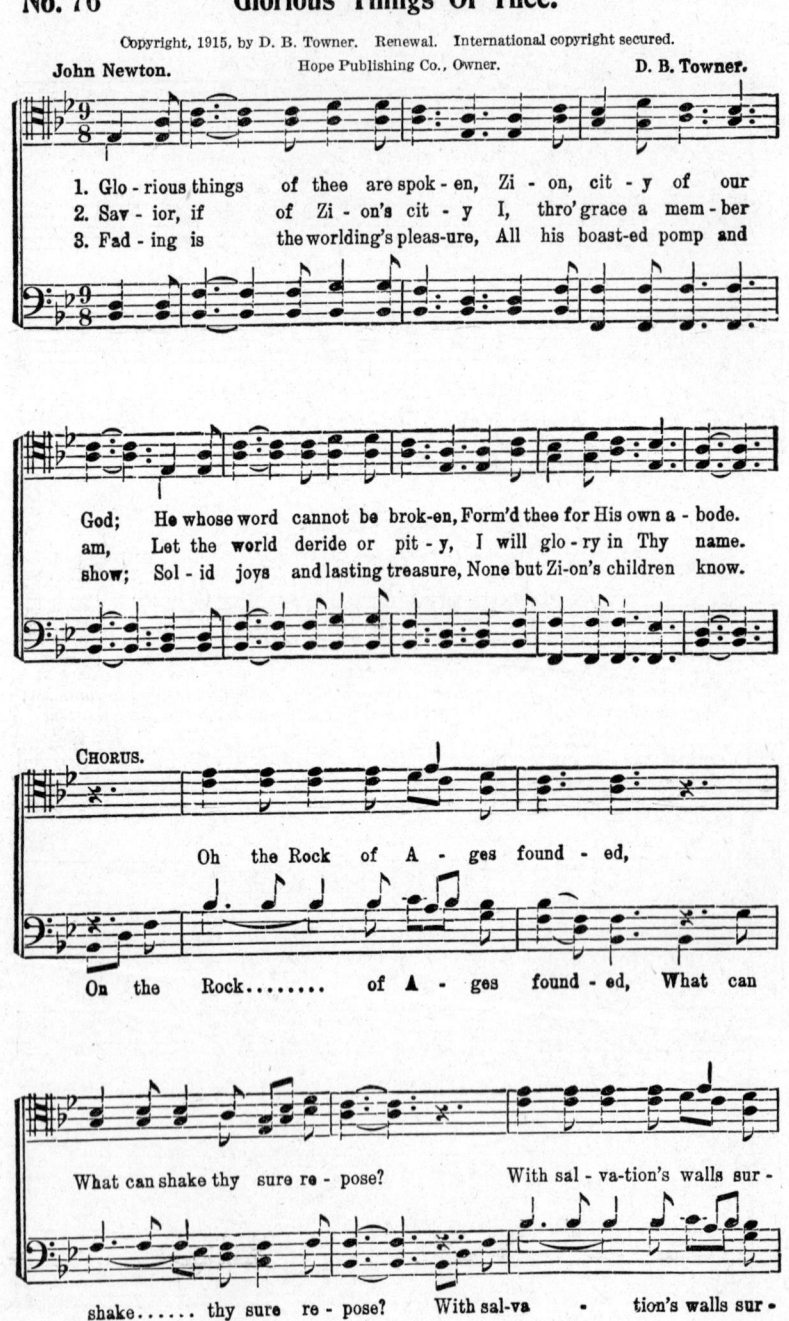

No. 76 Glorious Things Of Thee.

Copyright, 1915, by D. B. Towner. Renewal. International copyright secured.
Hope Publishing Co., Owner.

John Newton. D. B. Towner.

1. Glo - rious things of thee are spok - en, Zi - on, cit - y of our God; He whose word cannot be brok - en, Form'd thee for His own a - bode.
2. Sav - ior, if of Zi - on's cit - y I, thro' grace a mem - ber am, Let the world deride or pit - y, I will glo - ry in Thy name.
3. Fad - ing is the worlding's pleas - ure, All his boast - ed pomp and show; Sol - id joys and lasting treasure, None but Zi - on's children know.

CHORUS.

Oh the Rock of A - ges found - ed, What can shake thy sure re - pose? With sal - va - tion's walls sur-

On the Rock........ of A - ges found - ed, shake...... thy sure re - pose? With sal - va - tion's walls sur-

Glorious Things Of Thee. Concluded.

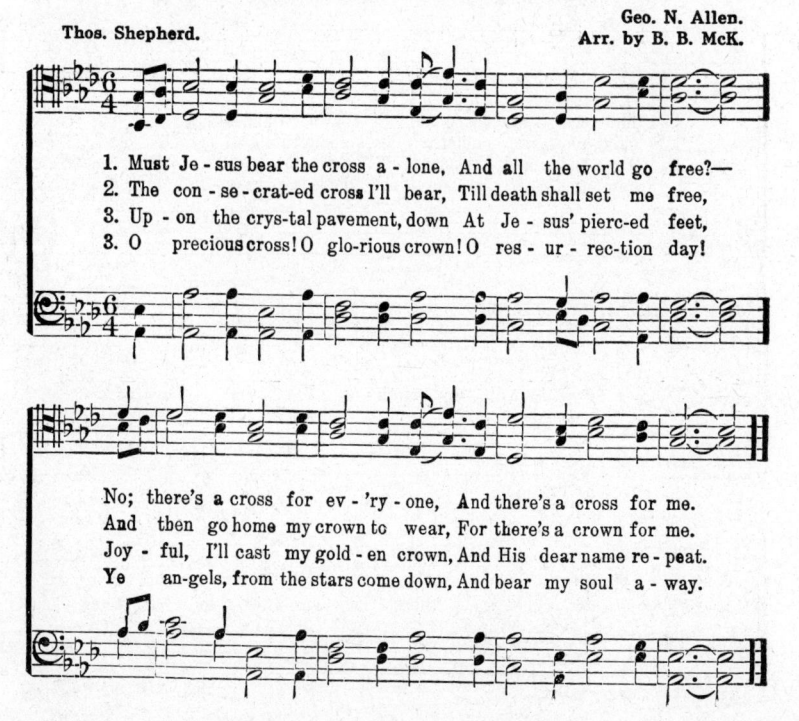

round - ed, Thou canst smile at all Thy foes, With sal-

round - ed, Thou canst smile....... at all Thy foes,

va - tion's wall sur-round-ed, Thou canst smile at all Thy foes.

No. 77   Must Jesus Bear The Cross Alone?

Thos. Shepherd.

Geo. N. Allen.
Arr. by B. B. McK.

1. Must Je-sus bear the cross a-lone, And all the world go free?—
2. The con-se-crat-ed cross I'll bear, Till death shall set me free,
3. Up - on the crys-tal pavement, down At Je-sus' pierc-ed feet,
3. O precious cross! O glo-rious crown! O res - ur - rec-tion day!

No; there's a cross for ev - 'ry - one, And there's a cross for me.
And then go home my crown to wear, For there's a crown for me.
Joy - ful, I'll cast my gold - en crown, And His dear name re - peat.
Ye an-gels, from the stars come down, And bear my soul a - way.

No. 78 Tell Mother I'll Be There.

Copyright, 1926, by Charles M. Fillmore. Renewal.

C. M. F.
Charles M. Fillmore.

SOLO. (*When instrument is used play Solo in treble clef.*)

1. When I was but a lit-tle child, how well I rec-ol-lect
2. Tho' I was oft-en way-ward, she was al-ways kind and good,
3. When I be-came a prod-i-gal and left the old roof-tree,
4. One day a mes-sage came to me, it bade me quick-ly come,

How I would grieve my moth-er by my fol-ly and neg-lect;
So pa-tient, gen-tle, lov-ing, when I act-ed rough and rude;
She al-most broke her lov-ing heart in mourn-ing af-ter me,
If I would see my moth-er ere the Sav-ior took her home;

And now that she has gone to heav'n, I miss her ten-der care:
My child-hood grief and tri-als, she would glad-ly with me share;
And day and night she prayed to God to keep me in His care:
I prom-ised her, be-fore she died, for heav-en to pre-pare:

O an-gels, tell my moth-er I'll be there....

CHORUS. (*Melody in Second Tenor.*)

Tell moth-er I'll be there, in an-swer to her payer, This

Tell Mother I'll Be There.

mes-sage, guardian an-gel, to her bear, Tell mother I'll be there, heav'n's joys with her to share, Yes, tell my dar-ling moth-er I'll be there.

No. 79 Jesus, Savior, Pilot Me.

E. Hopper.
J. E. Gould.

Melody in 2nd Tenor.

1. Je - sus, Sav - ior, pi - lot me O - ver life's tem - pes-tuous sea;
2. As a moth - er stills her child, Thou canst hush the o - cean wild;
3. When at last I near the shore, And the fear - ful break-ers roar

Un-known waves be - fore me roll, Hid - ing rock and treach'rous shoal;
Boist'rous waves o - bey Thy will When Thou say'st to them, "Be still!"
'Twixt me and the peaceful rest, Then, while lean-ing on Thy breast,

Chart and com-pass came from Thee; Je - sus, Sav - ior, pi - lot me.
Won-drous Sov-reign of the sea, Je - sus, Sav - ior, pi - lot me.
May I hear Thee say to me, "Fear not, I will pi - lot thee!"

No. 80   Nearer Home.

Alice Cary.   Arr. copyright, 1925, by Robert H. Coleman.   E. D. Keck.
Arr. B. B. McKinney.

1. O'er the hills the sun is set-ing, And the eve......... is drawing nigh,......... Slow-ly drops the gen-tle twi-light, For an-oth-er day is gone, a day is gone; Gone for aye,......... its race is o-ver, Soon the dark-'ning shades will come,......... Still 'tis sweet to know at eve-ning We are

2. One day near-er sings the sail-or, As he glides......... the wa-ters o'er,......... While the light is soft-ly dy-ing, On the dis-tant, na-tive shore, the na-tive shore; Thus the Chris-tian, on life's o-cean, As his light-boat cuts the foam,......... In the eve-ning cries with rap-ture, I am

3. Near-er home, yes, one day near-er, To our home......... be-yond the sky,......... To the green fields and the foun-tains, In our Father's home on high, His home on high; For the heav'ns...... are grow-ing bright-er, And the lamps......... hang in the dome,......... And our hearts are grow-ing light-er For we're

is drawing nigh, ... oth-er day is gone; ... gone for aye, its race is o-ver, Soon the dark'ning shades will come, shades will come,

Nearer Home.

CHORUS.

one day nearer home, one day nearer home. Near-er home, Near-er home,
one .... day nearer home ....
Near-er home, ... Nearer to our home on high, To the green fields
Near-er home,
and the foun-tains, Of a land beyond the sky, beyond the sky.
Of a land ....be-yond the sky ....

No. 81 Jesus, The Very Thought Of Thee.

Arr. copyright, 1925, by Robert H. Coleman.

Edward Caswall. Rev. J. B. Dykes.
Arr. B. B. McK.

1. Je - sus! the ver - y thought of Thee With sweetness fills my breast:
2. O hope of ev - 'ry con - trite heart, O joy of all the meek,
3. Je - sus, our on - ly joy be Thou, As Thou our prize shall be;

But sweeter far Thy face to see, And in Thy pres-ence rest.
To those who ask, how kind Thou art! How good to those who seek.
Je - sus, be Thou our glo - ry now, And thro' e - ter - ni - ty.

No. 82 Looking This Way.

Copyright, 1905, by J. W. Van DeVenter.
Copyright, 1911, by Charles H. Alexander. International copyright secured.
Hope Publishing Co., Owner.

J. W. V. J. W. Van DeVenter.

1. O-ver the riv-er fa-ces I see, Fair as the morn-ing, look-ing for me; Free from their sor-row, grief, and des-pair, Wait-ing and watch-ing pa-tient-ly there.
2. Fa-ther and moth-er safe in the vale, Watch for the boat-man, wait for the sail, Bear-ing the loved ones o-ver the tide, In-to the har-bor, near to their side.
3. Broth-er and sis-ter, gone to that clime, Wait for the oth-ers com-ing some time; Safe with the an-gels, whit-er than snow, Watching for dear ones wait-ing be-low.
4. Sweet lit-tle dar-ling, light of the home, Look-ing for some-one, beck-on-ing "Come!" Bright as a sun-beam, pure as the dew, Anx-ious-ly look-ing, moth-er, for you.
5. Je-sus the Sav-ior, Bright Morning Star, Look-ing for lost ones stray-ing a-far, Hear the glad mes-sage,—why will you roam? Je-sus is call-ing: "Sin-ner, come home!"

p ad lib.

CHORUS.

Look-ing this way, yes, look-ing this way, Loved ones are waiting, Looking this way; Fair as the morn-ing, bright as the day, Dear ones in glo-ry look-ing this way.

No. 83 Only Trust In Jesus.

Miss Pauline Sadler. Copyright, 1925, by Robert H. Coleman. B. B. McKinney.

1. When the way is dark and drear-y, And your path would lead astray,
2. When your heart is sad and lone-ly, And your grief is hard to bear,
3. Though temp-ta-tion come up-on you, Call-ing, call-ing day by day,
4. When your work on earth is o-ver, And you reach the riv-er wide,

If you'll on-ly trust in Je-sus, He will guide you all the way.
If you'll on-ly trust in Je-sus, He will all your sor-rows share.
If you'll on-ly trust in Je-sus, You can nev-er go a-stray.
Christ, the Sav-ior, will go with you, He will bear you o'er the tide.

CHORUS.

He'll go with you, He'll go with you, He'll go with you to the end........
to the end,

In your joy or in your sor-row, He will be your dearest Friend.

No. 84   Nearer, My God, To Thee.

S. F. Adams.   Lowell Mason.

1. Near-er, my God, to Thee, Near-er to Thee; E'en tho' it be a cross That rais-eth me; Still all my song shall be,
2. Tho' like the wan-der-er, Day-light all gone, Darkness be o-ver me, My rest a stone; Yet in my dreams I'd be,
3. There let the way ap-pear, Steps un-to heav'n; All that Thou send-est me, In mer-cy giv'n; An-gels to beck-on me,
4. Then, with my wak-ing tho'ts, Bright with Thy praise, Out of my sto-ny griefs Beth-el I'll raise; So by my woes to be,
5. Or if, on joy-ful wing, Cleav-ing the sky, Sun, moon and stars for-got, Up-ward I fly; Still all my song shall be,

Near-er, my God, to Thee! Near-er, my God, to Thee! Near-er to Thee!

No. 85   Holy Ghost! With Light Divine.

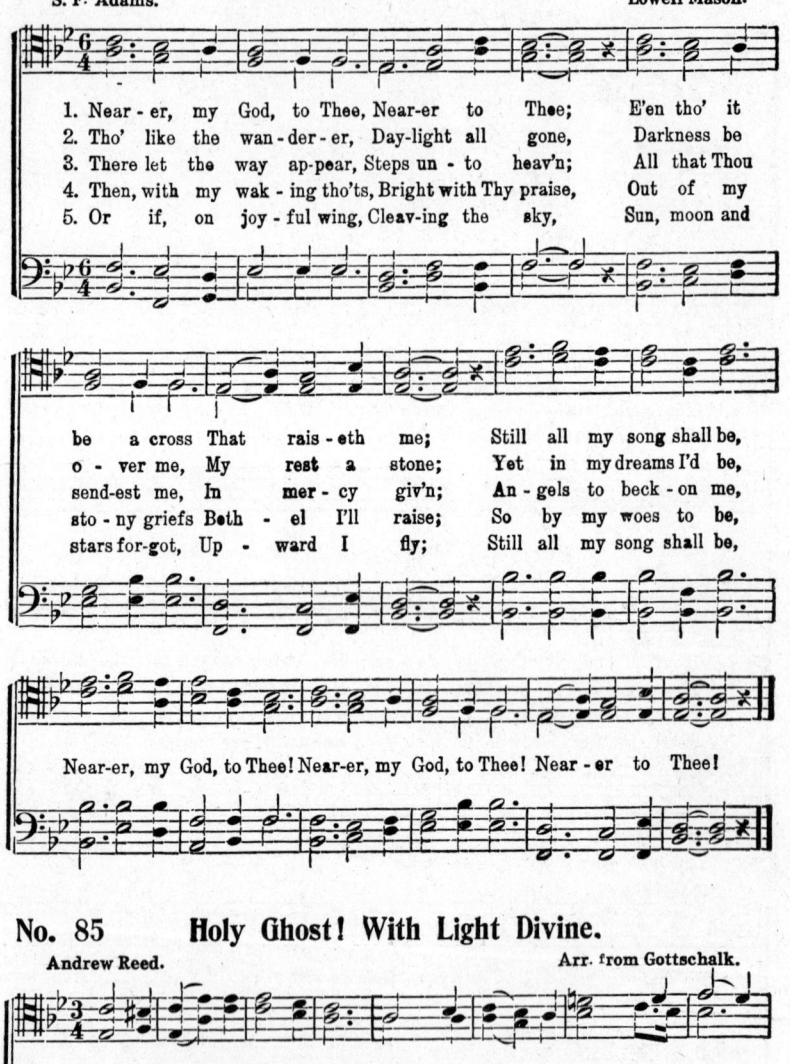

Andrew Reed.   Arr. from Gottschalk.

1. Ho-ly Ghost! with light divine, Shine up-on this heart of mine,
2. Ho-ly Ghost! with pow'r divine, Cleanse this guilt-y heart of mine,
3. Ho-ly Ghost! with joy di-vine, Cheer this sad-dened heart of mine,
4. Ho-ly Spir-it! all di-vine, Dwell with-in this heart of mine,

Holy Ghost! With Light Divine.

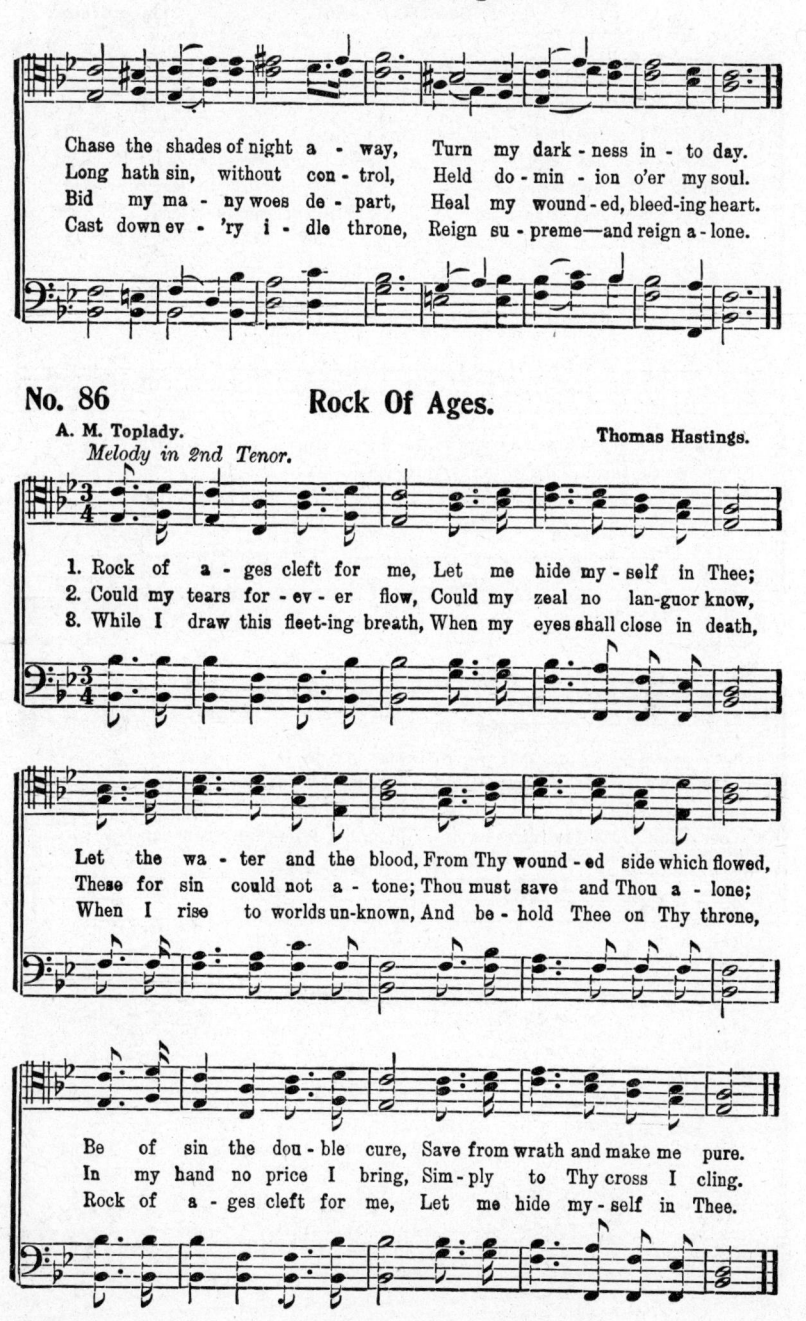

Chase the shades of night a - way, Turn my dark - ness in - to day.
Long hath sin, without con - trol, Held do - min - ion o'er my soul.
Bid my ma - ny woes de - part, Heal my wound - ed, bleed-ing heart.
Cast down ev - 'ry i - dle throne, Reign su - preme—and reign a - lone.

No. 86   **Rock Of Ages.**

A. M. Toplady.   Thomas Hastings.
Melody in 2nd Tenor.

1. Rock of a - ges cleft for me, Let me hide my - self in Thee;
2. Could my tears for - ev - er flow, Could my zeal no lan-guor know,
3. While I draw this fleet-ing breath, When my eyes shall close in death,

Let the wa - ter and the blood, From Thy wound - ed side which flowed,
These for sin could not a - tone; Thou must save and Thou a - lone;
When I rise to worlds un-known, And be - hold Thee on Thy throne,

Be of sin the dou - ble cure, Save from wrath and make me pure.
In my hand no price I bring, Sim - ply to Thy cross I cling.
Rock of a - ges cleft for me, Let me hide my - self in Thee.

No. 87 Silent Night! Holy Night!

CHRISTMAS CAROL.

Rev. Joseph Mohr.   Arr. copyright, 1925, by Rob't H. Coleman.   Arr. by B. B. McKinney.   Franz Gruber.

1. Si - lent night! Ho - ly night! All is dark, save the light
2. Si - lent night! Peace - ful night! Darkness flies, all is light;
3. Si - lent night! Ho - ly night! Guid-ing Star, lend thy light!
4. Si - lent night! Ho - liest night! Wondrous Star, lend thy light!

Yon - der where they sweet vig - ils keep, O'er the Babe who in si -
Shepherds hear the an - gels sing, "Al - le - lu - ia! hail
See the East - ern wise men bring Gifts and hom - age to
With the an - gels let us sing Al - le - lu - ia to

lent sleep Rests in heav-en - ly peace, Rests in heav - en - ly peace.
the King! Christ the Sav - ior born, Je-sus the Sav - ior is born.
our King! Christ the Sav - ior is born, Je-sus the Sav - ior is born.
our King! Christ the Sav - ior is born, Je-sus the Sav - ior is born.

No. 88 Asleep In Jesus.

Margaret Mackay.   Wm. B. Bradbury. Arr. I. E. R.

1. A-sleep in Je - sus! bless - ed sleep, From which none ever wakes to weep!
2. A-sleep in Je - sus! O how sweet To be for such a slum-ber meet!
3. A-sleep in Je - sus! peace-ful rest, Whose waking is su-preme-ly blest!

Asleep In Jesus.

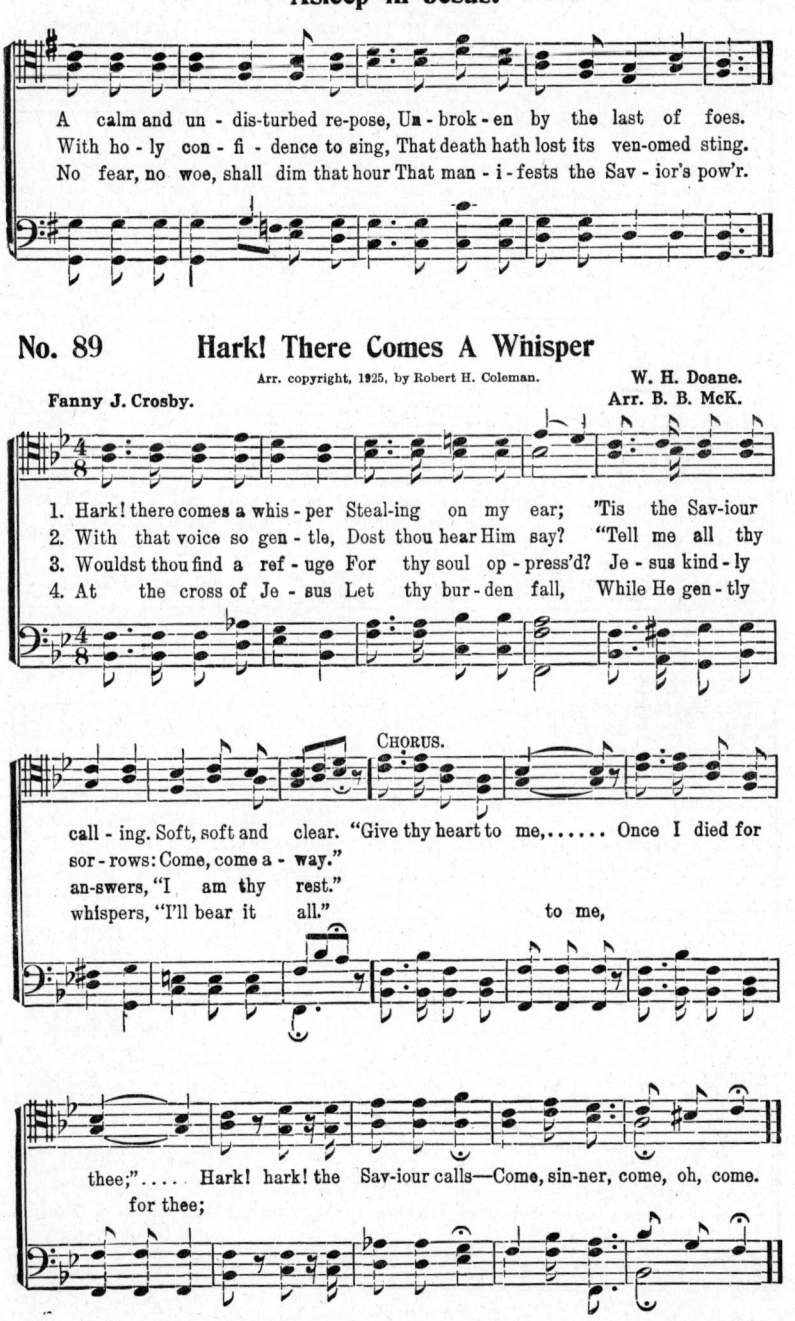

A calm and un-dis-turbed re-pose, Un-brok-en by the last of foes.
With ho-ly con-fi-dence to sing, That death hath lost its ven-omed sting.
No fear, no woe, shall dim that hour That man-i-fests the Sav-ior's pow'r.

No. 89 Hark! There Comes A Whisper

Arr. copyright, 1925, by Robert H. Coleman.

Fanny J. Crosby.
W. H. Doane.
Arr. B. B. McK.

1. Hark! there comes a whis-per Steal-ing on my ear; 'Tis the Sav-iour
2. With that voice so gen-tle, Dost thou hear Him say? "Tell me all thy
3. Wouldst thou find a ref-uge For thy soul op-press'd? Je-sus kind-ly
4. At the cross of Je-sus Let thy bur-den fall, While He gen-tly

CHORUS.

call-ing. Soft, soft and clear. "Give thy heart to me,...... Once I died for
sor-rows: Come, come a-way."
an-swers, "I am thy rest."
whis-pers, "I'll bear it all." to me,

thee;".... Hark! hark! the Sav-iour calls—Come, sin-ner, come, oh, come.
for thee;

No. 90 O Love That Will Not Let Me Go.

Arr. copyright 1925, by Robert H. Coleman.

George Matheson.
A. L. Peace.
Arr. B. B. McKinney.

1. O Love that will not let me go, I rest my wea-ry soul in Thee;...... I give Thee back the life I owe,...... That in Thine o-cean depths its flow May rich-er, full-er be.
2. O Light that fol-l'west all my way, I yield my flick'ring torch to Thee;...... My heart re-stores its bor-rowed ray,...... That in Thy sunshine's glow its day May bright-er, fair-er be.
3. O Joy that seekest me thro' pain, I can-not close my heart to Thee;...... I trace the rain-bow thro' the rain,...... And feel the prom-ise is not vain That morn shall tear-less be.
4. O Cross that lift-est up my head, I dare not ask to hide from Thee;...... I lay in dust life's glo-ry dead,...... And from the ground there blossoms red Life that shall end-less be.

No. 91 Sun Of My Soul, Thou Savior Dear.

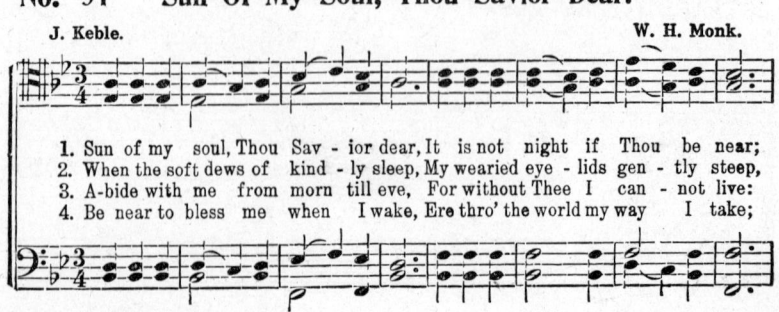

J. Keble.
W. H. Monk.

1. Sun of my soul, Thou Sav-ior dear, It is not night if Thou be near;
2. When the soft dews of kind-ly sleep, My wearied eye-lids gen-tly steep,
3. A-bide with me from morn till eve, For without Thee I can-not live:
4. Be near to bless me when I wake, Ere thro' the world my way I take;

Sun Of My Soul, Thou Savior Dear.

Oh, may no earth-born cloud a-rise, To hide Thee from Thy ser-vant's eyes.
Be my last tho't—how sweet to rest, For-ev-er on my Sav-ior's breast.
A-bide with me when night is nigh, For with-out Thee I dare not die.
A-bide with me till in Thy love, I lose my-self in heav'n a-bove.

No. 92 My Jesus, I Love Thee.

Arr. copyright, 1925, by Robert H. Coleman.

Anon.

A. J. Gordon.
Arr. by B. B. McKinney.

1. My Je-sus, I love Thee, I know Thou art mine, For Thee all the fol-lies of sin I re-sign; My gra-cious Re-deem-er, my Sav-ior art Thou; If ev-er I loved Thee, my Je-sus, 'tis now.
2. I love Thee, be-cause Thou hast first lov-ed me, And pur-chased my par-don on Cal-va-ry's tree; I love Thee for wear-ing the thorns on Thy brow: If ev-er I loved Thee, my Je-sus, 'tis now.
3. I'll love Thee in life, I will love Thee in death, And praise Thee as long as Thou lend-est me breath; And say when the death-dew lies cold on my brow, If ev-er I loved Thee, my Je-sus, 'tis now.
4. In man-sions of glo-ry and end-less de-light, I'll ev-er a-dore Thee in heav-en so bright; I'll sing with the glit-ter-ing crown on my brow, If ev-er I loved Thee, my Je-sus, 'tis now.

No. 93 The Lord Is My Shepherd.

James Montgomery.
Copyright, 1932, by E. O. Sellers.
Ernest O. Sellers.
Arr. from Meyer.

1. The Lord is my Shepherd, no want shall I know; I feed in green pastures, safe-folded I rest; He leadeth my soul where the still waters flow, Restores me when wand'ring, redeems when oppressed, Restores me when wand'ring, redeems when oppressed.
2. Thro' the valley and shadow of death tho' I stray, Since Thou art my guardian no evil I fear; Thy rod shall defend me, Thy staff be my stay; No harm can be-fall, with my Comforter near, No harm can be-fall with my Comforter near.
3. In midst of affliction my table is spread, With blessings unmeasured my cup runneth o'er; With perfume and oil Thou anointest my head, O what shall I ask of Thy providence more? O what shall I ask of Thy providence more.

No. 94 Holy Spirit, Faithful Guide.

Marcus M. Wells.
Arr. copyright, 1932, by E. O. Sellers.
Ernest O. Sellers.
Adopted from the German.

1. Holy Spirit, faithful Guide, Ever near the Christian's side; Gently lead us by the hand, Pilgrims in a desert land;
2. Ever present, truest Friend, Ever near Thine aid to lend, Leave us not to doubt and fear, Groping on in darkness drear;
3. When our days of toil shall cease, Waiting still for sweet release, Nothing left but heav'n and pray'r, Wond'ring if our names are there.

Holy Spirit, Faithful Guide. Concluded.

Wea-ry souls for-e'er re-joice, While they hear that sweet-est
When the storms are rag-ing sore, Hearts grow faint and hopes give
Wad-ing deep the dis-mal flood, Pleading naught but Je-sus'

voice, Whisp'ring softly, "Wand'rer, come! Fol-low Me, I'll guide thee home."
o'er, Whis-per softly, "Wand'rer, come! Fol-low Me, I'll guide thee home."
blood, Whis-per softly, "Wand'rer, come! Fol-low Me, I'll guide thee home."

No. 95 The Day Is Past And Over.

Antolius (7th Cent.)
J. M. Neale, Tr.
Copyright, 1932, by E. O. Sellers.
Ernest O. Sellers.

1. The day is past and o-ver; All thanks O Lord to Thee; We pray Thee
2. The joys of day are o-ver; We lift our hearts to Thee; And call on
3. The toils of day are o-ver; We raise the hymn to Thee; And ask that

that of-fence-less The hours of dark may be. O Je-sus
Thee that sin-less The hours of gloom may be.
free from per-il The hours of fear may be. O Je-sus

keep us in Thy sight, And save us through the com-ing night.
make their dark-ness light, And save us through the com-ing night.
keep us in Thy sight, And guard us through the com-ing night.

No. 96   My Country, 'Tis Of Thee.

S. F. Smith.   AMERICA.   English. Arr. I. E. R.

1. My country! 'tis of thee, Sweet land of lib-er-ty, Of thee I sing; Land where my father's died, Land of the pilgrim's pride, From ev'ry mountain side, Let freedom ring.
2. My na-tive country thee, Land of the noble, free, Thy name I love; I love thy rocks and rills, Thy woods and templed hills, My heart with rapture thrills, Like that a-bove.
3. Let music swell the breeze, And ring from all the trees, Sweet freedom's song; Let mortal tongues awake, Let all that breathe partake, Let rocks their silence break, The sound prolong.
4. Our father's God! to Thee, Author of lib-er-ty, To Thee we sing; Long may our land be bright, With freedom's holy light, Protect us by Thy might, Great God, our King!

No. 97   More Love To Thee.

Mrs. E. P. Prentice.   Copyright, 1870, by W. H. Doane.   W. H. Doane.

1. More love to Thee, O Christ! More love to Thee! Hear Thou the pray'r I make, On bend-ed knee; This is my earn-est plea:
2. Once earth-ly joy I craved, Sought peace and rest; Now Thee a-lone I seek, Give what is best; This all my pray'r shall be:
3. Let sor-row do its work, Send grief and pain, Sweet are Thy mes-sen-gers, Sweet their re-frain, When they can sing with me:
4. Then shall my la-test breath Whis-per Thy praise, This be the part-ing cry My heart shall raise, This still its pray'r shall be;

More Love To Thee.

More love, O Christ, to Thee, More love to Thee, More love to Thee.

No. 98   Be A Man.

I. E. R.   Copyright, 1917, by Robert H. Coleman.   I. E. Reynolds.

1. As you bat-tle on thro' life, Be a man, be a man; God will help you in the strife, Be a man, be a man.
2. Stand for God and for the right, Be a man, be a man; Sa-tan's host for-ev-er fight, Be a man, be a man.
3. Christ, our Cap-tain, gives command, Be a man, be a man; Struggle on, is His de-mand, Be a man, be a man.
4. A re-ward a-waits you there, Be a man, be a man; You'll your Captain's glo-ry share, Be a man, be a man.

CHORUS.

Be a man, be a man, Be a man, be a man, *rit.* Stand for Christ and brave-ly fight, Be a man, be a man.

No. 99 I Love Him.

London Hymn Book. Arr. copyright, 1932, by Robert H. Coleman. **Arr. B. B. McKinney.**
Melody in low bass, other parts humming.

1. Gone from my heart the world and all its charm; Gone are my sins and all that would a-larm; Gone ev-er-more, and by His grace I know
2. Once I was lost up-on the plains of sin; Once was a slave to doubts and fears with-in; Once was a-fraid to trust a lov-ing God,
3. Once I was bound, but now I am set free; Once I was blind, but now the light I see; Once I was dead, but now in Christ I live,

Fine. **CHORUS.**

The precious blood of Jesus cleanses white as snow.
But now my guilt is washed away in Je-sus' blood. I love Him,
To tell the world the peace that He a-lone can give.

D. S.—And purchased my sal-va-tion on Cal-v'ry's tree.

I love Him,...... I love Him,...... I love Him, Because He first loved me,..... loved me,

No. 100 Stars Of The Summer Night.

H. W. Longfellow. **I. B. Woodbury.**
Slow and gentle.

1. Stars of the summer night! Far in yon azure deeps, Hide, hide your golden light;
2. Moon of the summer night! Far down yon western steeps, Sink, sink in si-lent light;
3. Dreams of the summer night! Tell her, her lover keeps Watch, while in slumbers light;

Stars Of The Summer Night.

She sleeps! my la - dy sleeps! She sleeps! she sleeps! my la - dy sleeps!

No. 101 Lead, Kindly Light.

J. H. Newman. J. B. Dykes. Arr. by H. F.

Melody in Second Tenor.

1. Lead, kind-ly Light! a - mid th' en-cir-cling gloom, Lead Thou me on. The night is dark, and I am far from home: Lead Thou me on. Keep Thou my feet; I do not ask to see...... The dis - tant scene; one step e - nough for me.
2. I was not ev - er thus, nor prayed that Thou Shouldst lead me on. I loved to choose and see my path; but now Lead Thou me on. I loved the gar - ish day, and, spite of fears,.... Pride ruled my will, Re-mem-ber not past years.
3. So long Thy pow'r hath blest me, sure it still Will lead me on. O'er moor and fen, o'er crag and tor-rent, till The night is gone; And with the morn those an - gel fa - ces smile,.... Which I have loved long since, and lost a - while.

No. 102 The Secret Place.

B. B. McK. Copyright, 1932, by Robert H. Coleman. B. B. McKinney.

1. When my heart is filled with sad-ness, And I'm sink-ing in de-spair,
2. When the tempter would en-thrall me By some sin-ful, hid-den snare;
3. Oh, the bless-ed, sweet com-mun-ion, As I oft-en lin-ger there;

Je-sus gives me peace and glad-ness, In the se-cret place of pray'r.
I can hear my Sav-iour call me, To the se-cret place of pray'r.
Oh, the joy of such a un-ion, In the se-cret place of pray'r.

CHORUS

In the se-cret place of pray'r, There is joy be-yond com-pare;

All the burdens roll from my troubled soul, In the se-cret place of pray'r.

No 103 Where Will You Spend Eternity?

Arr. copyright, 1928, by Robert H. Coleman.

E. A. Hoffman. J. H. Tenney. Arr. by B. B. McKinney.

1. Where will you spend e-ter-ni-ty? This question comes to you and me!
2. Man-y are choosing Christ to-day, Turn-ing from all their sins a-way;
3. Re-pent, believe, this ver-y hour, Trust in the Saviour's grace and pow'r.

Where Will You Spend Eternity? Concluded.

Tell me, what shall your answer be? Where will you spend e-ter-ni-ty?
Heav'n shall their happy portion be; Where will you spend e-ter-ni-ty?
Then will your joy-ous an-swer be, Saved thro' a long e-ter-ni-ty!

1-2. E-ter-ni-ty! e-ter-ni-ty! Where will you spend e-ter-ni-ty?
3. E-ter-ni-ty! e-ter-ni-ty! Saved thro' a long e-ter-ni-ty!

No. 104 Shall We Meet?

Arr. copyright, 1932, by Robert H. Coleman.

H. L. Hastings.
Elihu Rice.
Arr. by B. B. McKinney.

1. Shall we meet be-yond the riv-er, Where the surg-es cease to roll;
2. Shall we meet be-yond the riv-er, When our storm-y voyage is o'er?
3. Shall we meet in yon-der cit-y, Where the tow'rs of crys-tal shine;
4. Shall we meet with Christ, our Saviour, When He comes to claim His own?

Where in all the bright for-ev-er, Sor-row ne'er shall press the soul?
Shall we meet and cast the an-chor By the bright ce-les-tial shore?
Where the walls are all of jas-per, Built by work-man-ship di-vine?
Shall we know His bless-ed fa-vor, And sit down up-on His throne?

FINE.

D. S.—Shall we meet be-yond the riv-er, Where the surg-es cease to roll?

CHORUS.   D. S.

Shall we meet,.... shall we meet,.... Shall we meet beyond the riv-er?
Shall we meet, shall we meet,

No. 105 Some Morning.

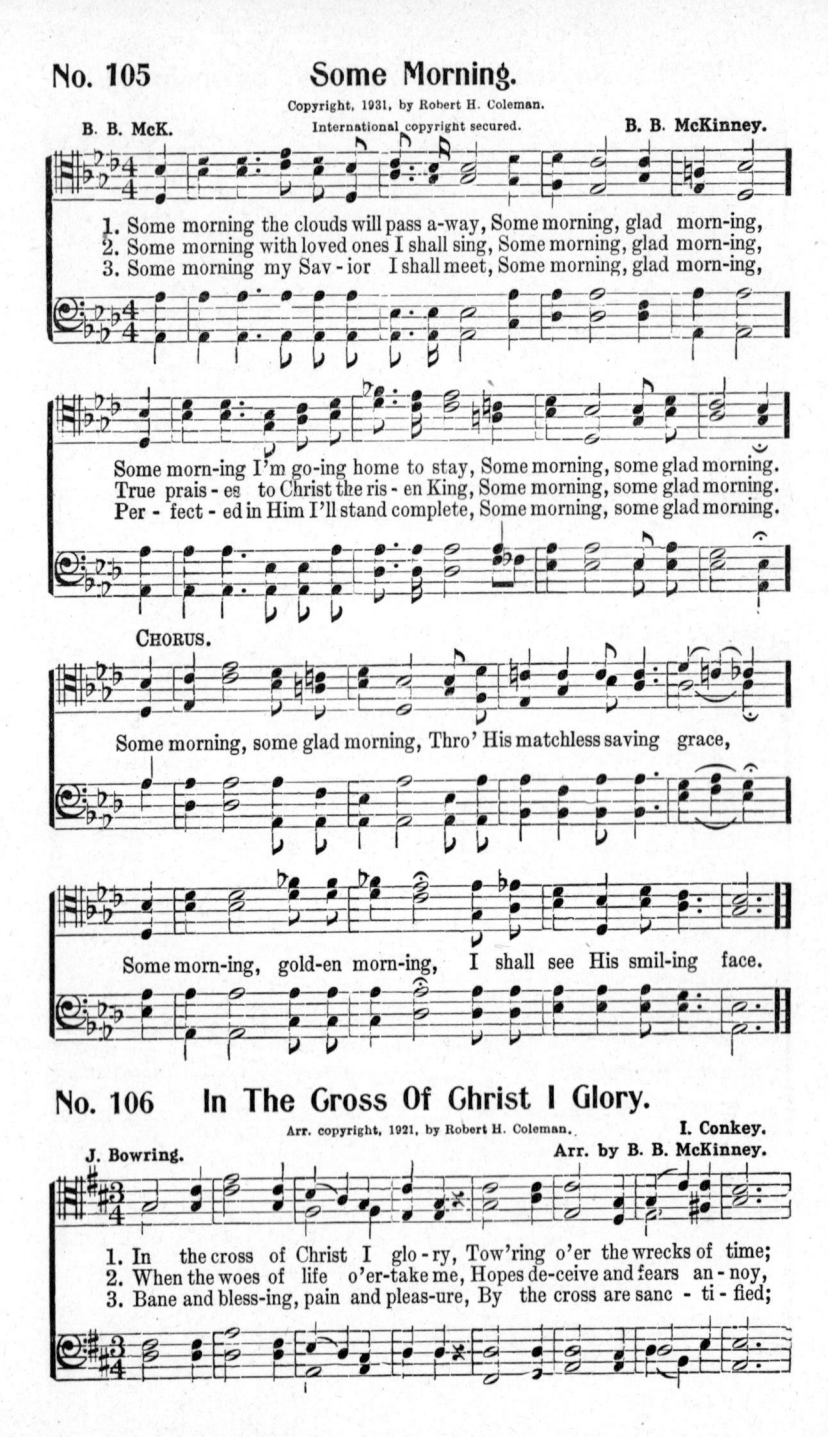

Copyright, 1931, by Robert H. Coleman.
International copyright secured.

B. B. McK.
B. B. McKinney.

1. Some morning the clouds will pass a-way, Some morning, glad morn-ing,
2. Some morning with loved ones I shall sing, Some morning, glad morn-ing,
3. Some morning my Sav-ior I shall meet, Some morning, glad morn-ing,

Some morn-ing I'm go-ing home to stay, Some morning, some glad morning.
True prais-es to Christ the ris-en King, Some morning, some glad morning.
Per-fect-ed in Him I'll stand complete, Some morning, some glad morning.

CHORUS.

Some morning, some glad morning, Thro' His matchless saving grace,

Some morn-ing, gold-en morn-ing, I shall see His smil-ing face.

No. 106 In The Cross Of Christ I Glory.

Arr. copyright, 1921, by Robert H. Coleman.

J. Bowring.
I. Conkey.
Arr. by B. B. McKinney.

1. In the cross of Christ I glo-ry, Tow'ring o'er the wrecks of time;
2. When the woes of life o'er-take me, Hopes de-ceive and fears an-noy,
3. Bane and bless-ing, pain and pleas-ure, By the cross are sanc-ti-fied;

In The Cross Of Christ I Glory. Concluded.

All the light of sa - cred sto - ry Gath-ers round its head sub-lime.
Nev - er shall the cross for - sake me; Lo! it glows with peace and joy.
Peace is there, that knows no meas-ure, Joys that thro' all time a - bide.

No. 107 The Many Mansions.

Copyright, 1931, by Robert H. Coleman.
International copyright secured.

B. B. McKinney. Arr. by B. B. McKinney.

1. Do not let your heart be troub - led, Nei - ther let it be a - fraid,
2. He has left the Ho - ly Spir - it, As our com-fort-er and guide,
3. Do not let your heart be troub - led, Toils of life will soon be o'er,

Lean up - on the pre - cious prom - ise That the bless-ed Mas-ter made.
Till He comes a - gain in glo - ry, With His loved ones to a - bide.
Then with Christ the bless-ed Sav - ior, We shall dwell for - ev - er - more.

CHORUS.

"In my Father's house are many mansions," If it were not so I would have told you;

"In my Father's house are many mansions," And all the streets are paved with gold.

No. 108 God Will Take Care Of You.

C. D. Martin. Copyright, 1905, by John A. Davis. Used by permission. W. S. Martin.

1. Be not dis - mayed what-e'er betide, God will take care of you;
2. Thro' days of toil when heart doth fail, God will take care of you;
3. All you may need He will pro - vide, God will take care of you;
4. No mat - ter what may be the test, God will take care of you,

Be - neath His wings of love a - bide, God will take care of you.
When dan-gers fierce your path as-sail, God will take care of you.
Noth - ing you ask will be de - nied, God will take care of you.
Lean, wear-y one, up - on His breast, God will take care of you.

CHORUS.

God will take care of you, Thro' ev - 'ry day, O'er all the way;

rit.

He will take care of you, God will take care of you......
take care of you.

No. 109 Jesus Calls Us.

Mrs. Cecil F. Alexander. William H. Jude. Arr. I. E. R.

1. Je - sus calls us o'er the tu - mult Of our life's wild restless sea,
2. Je - sus calls us from the wor - ship Of the vain world's golden store,
3. In our joys and in our sor - rows, Days of toil and hours of ease,
4. Je - sus calls us: by Thy mer - cies, Sav-iour, may we hear Thy call,

Jesus Calls Us. Concluded.

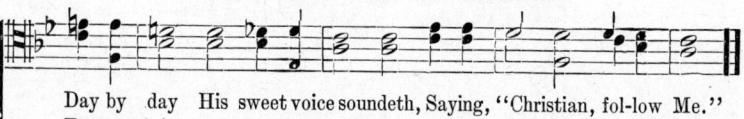

Day by day His sweet voice soundeth, Saying, "Christian, fol-low Me."
From each i - dol that would keep us, Saying, "Christian, love Me more."
Still He calls in cares and pleas-ures, "Christian, love Me more than these."
Give our hearts to Thy o - be-dience, Serve and love Thee best of all.

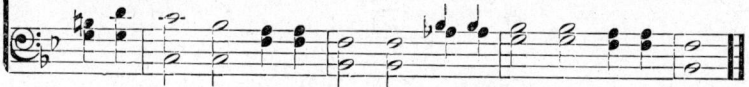

No. 110 The Shadows Of The Evening.

Adelaide Proctor. Copyright, 1932, by Robert H. Coleman. **H. W. Jeneson.**

1. The sha-dows of the ev'ning hours Fall from the dark'ning sky; Upon the fragrance of the flow'rs The dews of eve-ning lie. Before Thy throne, O Lord of Heav'n, We kneel at close of day; Look on Thy children from on high, And hear us while we pray.

2. The sor-rows of Thy servants, Lord, O do Thou not despise, But let the incense of our pray'rs, Be-fore Thy mer-cy rise. The brightness of the com-ing night Up-on the darkness rolls; With hopes of future glory chase The shadows from our souls.

3. Slow-ly the rays of daylight fade; So fade within our heart; The hopes in earthly love and joy, That one by one de-part. Slowly the bright stars one by one With-in the heavens shine; Give us, O Lord, fresh hopes in heav'n, And trust in things di-vine.

4. Let peace, O Lord, Thy peace, O God, Upon our souls descend; From mid-night fears and per-ils, Thou our trembling fears defend. Give us a re-spite from our toil; Calm and subdue our woes; Thro' the long day we labor, Lord, O give us now re - pose.

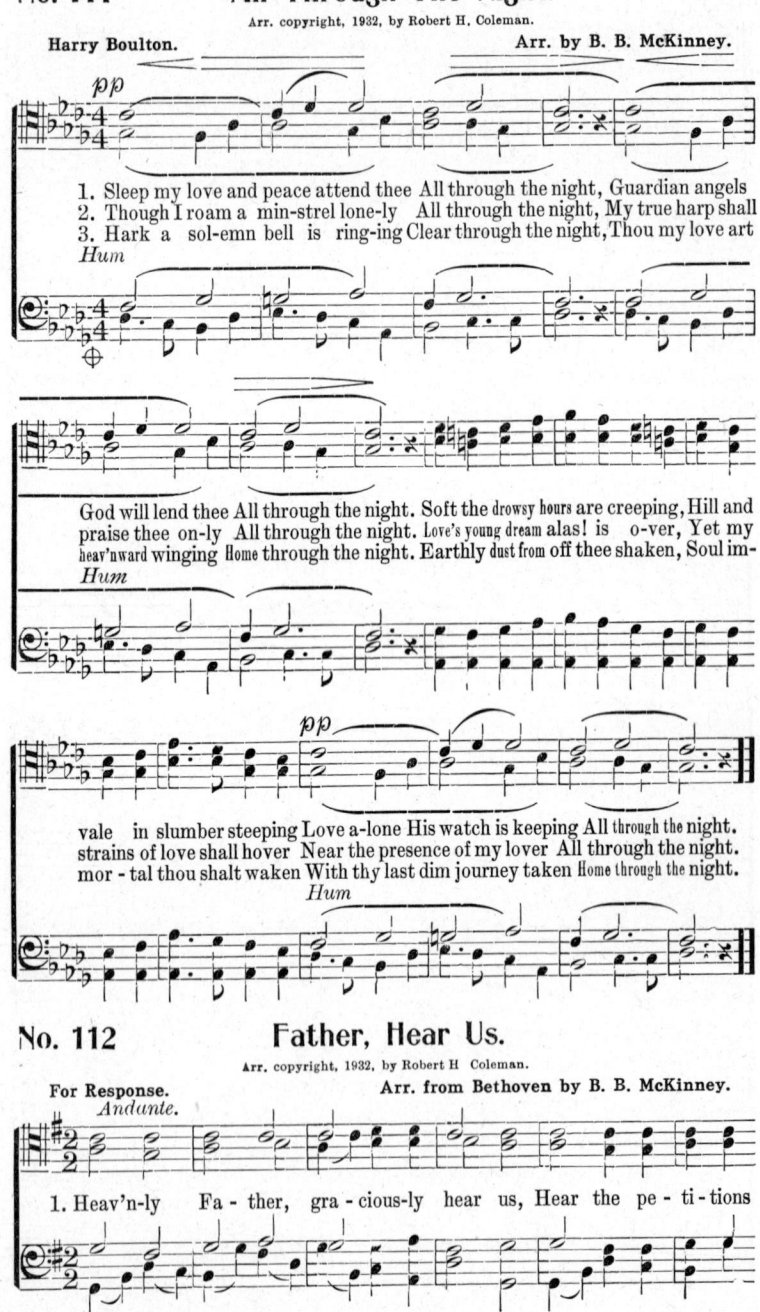

No. 111 — All Through The Night.

Arr. copyright, 1932, by Robert H. Coleman.

Harry Boulton.   Arr. by B. B. McKinney.

1. Sleep my love and peace attend thee All through the night, Guardian angels God will lend thee All through the night. Soft the drowsy hours are creeping, Hill and vale in slumber steeping Love a-lone His watch is keeping All through the night.
2. Though I roam a min-strel lone-ly All through the night, My true harp shall praise thee on-ly All through the night. Love's young dream alas! is o-ver, Yet my strains of love shall hover Near the presence of my lover All through the night.
3. Hark a sol-emn bell is ring-ing Clear through the night, Thou my love art heav'nward winging Home through the night. Earthly dust from off thee shaken, Soul immor-tal thou shalt waken With thy last dim journey taken Home through the night.

Hum

No. 112 — Father, Hear Us.

Arr. copyright, 1932, by Robert H Coleman.

For Response.   Arr. from Bethoven by B. B. McKinney.
Andante.

1. Heav'n-ly Fa-ther, gra-cious-ly hear us, Hear the pe-ti-tions

Father, Hear Us. Concluded.

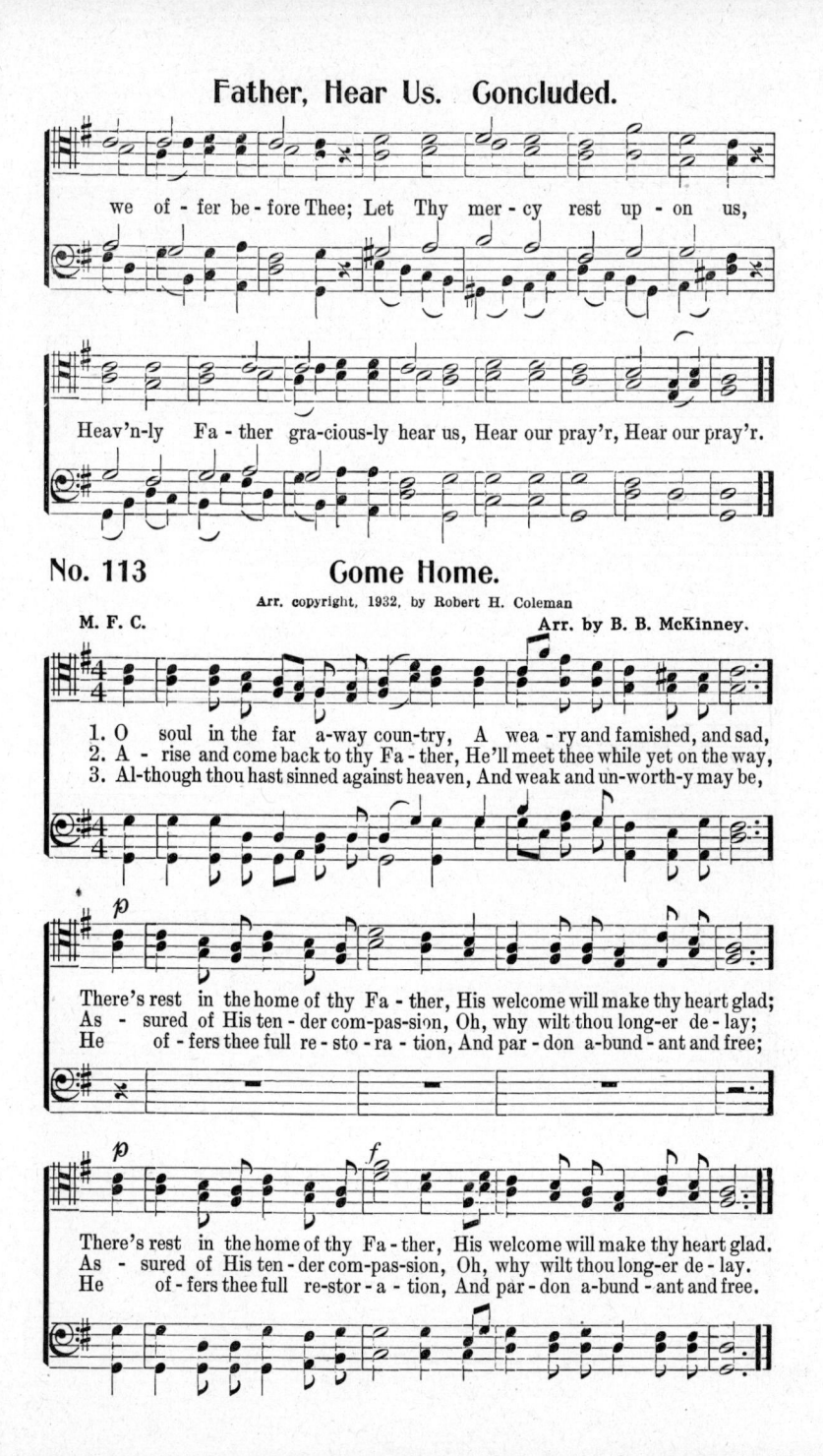

we of-fer be-fore Thee; Let Thy mer-cy rest up-on us,

Heav'n-ly Fa-ther gra-cious-ly hear us, Hear our pray'r, Hear our pray'r.

No. 113 **Come Home.**

Arr. copyright, 1932, by Robert H. Coleman

M. F. C.   Arr. by B. B. McKinney.

1. O soul in the far a-way coun-try, A wea-ry and famished, and sad,
2. A-rise and come back to thy Fa-ther, He'll meet thee while yet on the way,
3. Al-though thou hast sinned against heaven, And weak and un-worth-y may be,

There's rest in the home of thy Fa-ther, His welcome will make thy heart glad;
As-sured of His ten-der com-pas-sion, Oh, why wilt thou long-er de-lay;
He of-fers thee full re-sto-ra-tion, And par-don a-bund-ant and free;

There's rest in the home of thy Fa-ther, His welcome will make thy heart glad.
As-sured of His ten-der com-pas-sion, Oh, why wilt thou long-er de-lay.
He of-fers thee full re-stor-a-tion, And par-don a-bund-ant and free.

No. 114 Blessed Is He That Readeth.

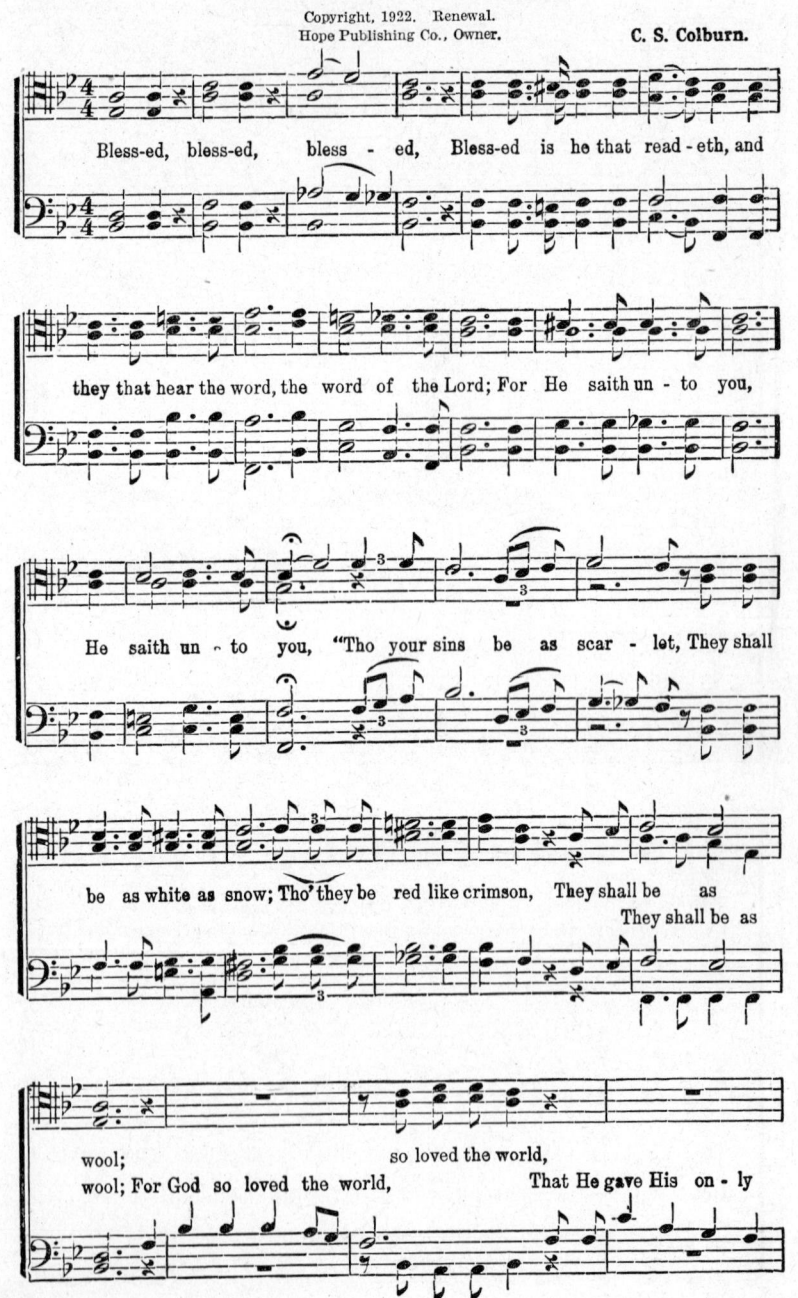

Copyright, 1922. Renewal.
Hope Publishing Co., Owner.

C. S. Colburn.

Bless-ed, bless-ed, bless - ed, Bless-ed is he that read-eth, and they that hear the word, the word of the Lord; For He saith un-to you, He saith un - to you, "Tho' your sins be as scar - let, They shall be as white as snow; Tho' they be red like crimson, They shall be as

They shall be as wool; so loved the world,

wool; For God so loved the world, That He gave His on - ly

Blessed Is He That Readeth.

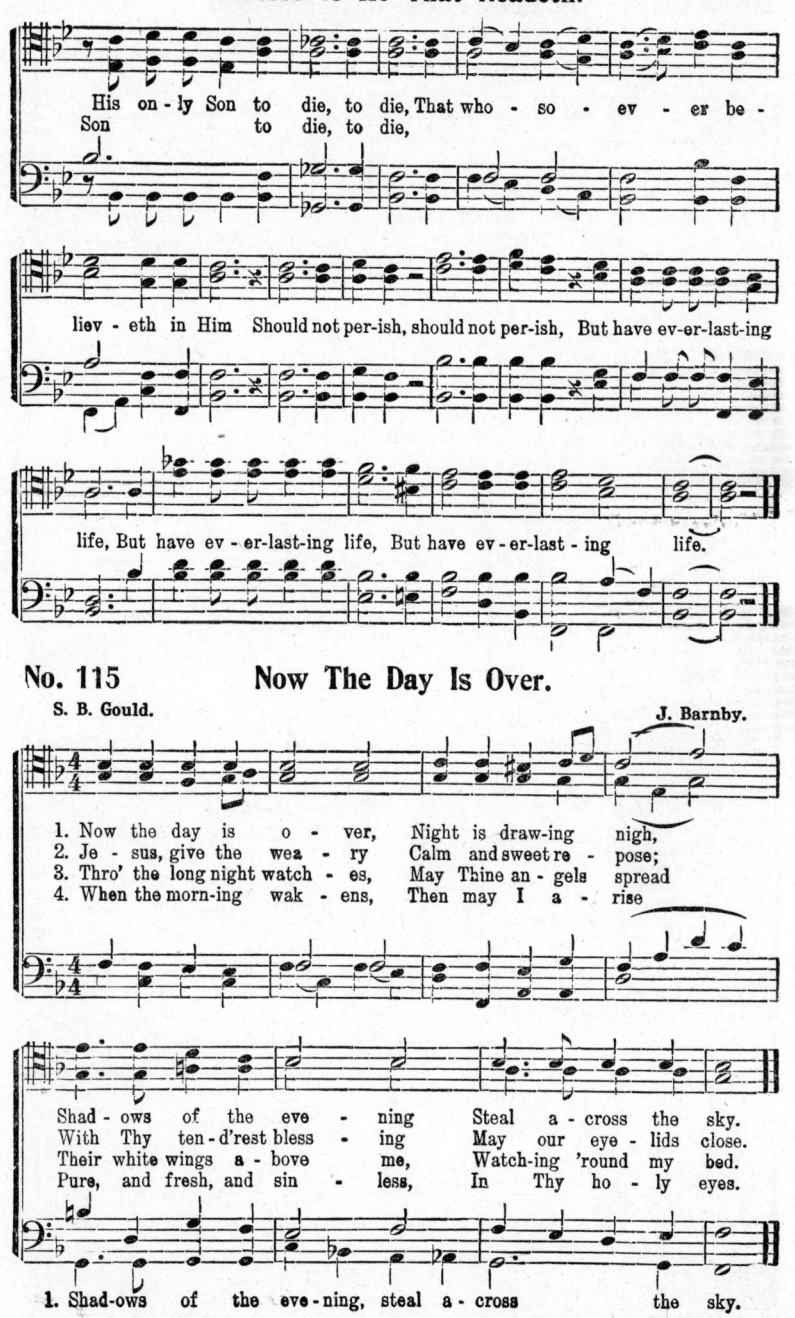

His on-ly Son to die, to die, That who-so-ev-er be-
Son to die, to die,

liev-eth in Him Should not per-ish, should not per-ish, But have ev-er-last-ing

life, But have ev-er-last-ing life, But have ev-er-last-ing life.

No. 115 Now The Day Is Over.

S. B. Gould.   J. Barnby.

1. Now the day is o - ver, Night is draw-ing nigh,
2. Je - sus, give the wea - ry Calm and sweet re - pose;
3. Thro' the long night watch - es, May Thine an - gels spread
4. When the morn-ing wak - ens, Then may I a - rise

Shad-ows of the eve - ning Steal a-cross the sky.
With Thy ten-d'rest bless - ing May our eye-lids close.
Their white wings a - bove me, Watch-ing 'round my bed.
Pure, and fresh, and sin - less, In Thy ho - ly eyes.

1. Shad-ows of the eve-ning, steal a-cross the sky.

No. 116   Tell Me The Old, Old Story.

As arranged for and sung by the Bel-Canto Quartet, Dallas, Texas.

Kate Hankey.   Arr. copyright, 1932, by Robert H. Coleman.   Arr. By Lawrence Bolton.   W. H. Doane.

1. Tell me the Old, Old Sto - ry, Of unseen things a - bove, Of Je - sus and His glo - ry, Of Je - sus and His love; Tell me the sto - ry sim - ply, As to a lit - tle child, For I am weak and wea - ry, And help - less and de - filed.
2. Tell me the sto - ry slow - ly, Thau I may take it in— That won-der-ful re - demp-tion, God's rem - e - dy for sin; Tell me the sto - ry oft - en, For I for - get so soon, The "ear-ly dew" of morn - ing Has passed a-way at noon.
3. Tell me the same old sto - ry, When you have cause to fear That this world's emp-ty glo - ry Is cost-ing me too dear; Yes, and when that world's glo - ry Is dawn-ing on my soul, Tell me the Old, Old Sto - ry: "Christ Je - sus makes thee whole.

CHORUS.

Tell me the Old, Old Sto - ry, Tell me the Old, Old Sto - ry, Tell me the Old, Old Sto - ry Of Je - sus and His love. A-men.

No. 117   We'll Never Say Good-bye.

Arr. copyright, 1932, by Robert H. Coleman

Mrs. . E. W. Chapman.
J. H. Tenney.
Arr. by B. B. McKinney.

1. Our friends on earth we meet with pleasure, While swift the moments fly,
2. How joy-ful is the tho't that lin-gers, When loved ones cross death's sea,
3. No part-ing words shall e'er be spok-en In that bright land of flow'rs,

Yet ev-er comes the tho't of sad-ness That we must say good-bye.
That when our la-bors here are end-ed, With them we'll ev-er be.
But songs of joy, and peace, and gladness, Shall ev-er-more be ours.

CHORUS.

We'll nev-er say good-bye in heav'n, We'll nev-er say good-bye; ....
good-bye;

Repeat chorus pp

For in that land of joy and song, We'll nev-er say good-bye.

No. 118 One Sweetly Solemn Thought.

Arr. copyright, 1821, by Rob't H. Coleman.

Phœbe Cary. R. S. Ambrose. Arr. by B. B. McKinney.

One Sweetly Solemn Thought.

Near-er leav-ing the cross,.... Near-er gain-ing the crown.

But ly-ing dark-ly be-tween, Winding a-down thro' the night

Is the si-lent unknown stream That leads at last to the light.

Fa-ther be near when my feet Are slip-ping o'er the brink,

rit.

For it may be, I am near-er home, Near-er now than I think.

No. 119   **No Shadows Yonder.**

Arr. copyright, 1928, by Robert H. Coleman.

Alfred R. Gaul. Arr. by B. B. McKinney.

No shad-ows yon - der, All light and song, Each day I won - der,

And say, "How long Shall time me sun - der From that dear throng?"

mf Tenor Solo.

No weep-ing yon - der; All fled a - way!

simile.

While here I wan - der Each wea-ry day......

Note:—Accompaniment may be played from these scores, but better results will be obtained from the "Holy City."

No Shadows Yonder. Concluded.

And sigh as I ponder My long, long stay.

No parting yonder, Time and space Never again shall sever,

Hearts cannot sever; Dearer and fonder Hands clasp forever;

None waiting yonder, Bought by the Lamb, All gathered under

The evergreen palm, Loud as night's thunder Ascends the glad psalm.

No. 120 No Burdens Yonder.

Copyright, 1906 and 1912, by Charles M. Alexander. International copyright secured.
Hope Publishing Co., Owner.

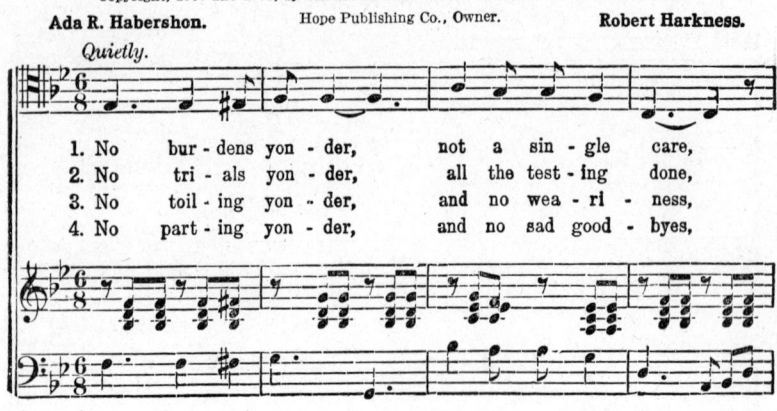

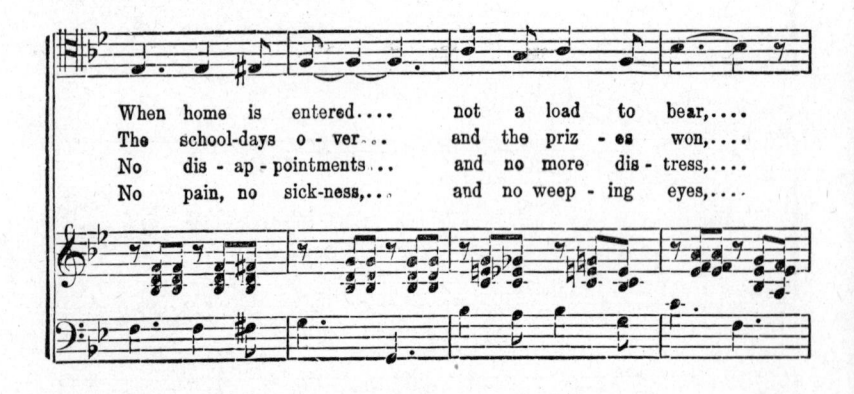

Ada R. Habershon. Robert Harkness.

Quietly.

1. No burdens yonder, not a single care, When home is entered.... not a load to bear,.... No burdens yonder, all will be laid down, Be-
2. No trials yonder, all the testing done, The school-days over... and the prizes won,.... No much-tried faith like gold in furnace heat, The
3. No toiling yonder, and no weariness, No disappointments... and no more distress,.... The future bright, the past all understood, We'll
4. No parting yonder, and no sad good-byes, No pain, no sickness,... and no weeping eyes,.... But best of all my Savior I shall see, No

No Burdens Yonder.

fore we share His glo - ry and His throne....
pu - ri - fy - ing will all be com - plete.....
see that all the way He led was good.....
cloud will come be - tween my Lord and me.....

CHORUS.

No bur-dens yon-der, All sorrows past, No bur-dens yon-der, Home at last...... at last.

* If a repetition of the chorus is desired, sing following measure and a half as written, otherwise pass to 2nd ending.

No. 121 **I Could'nt Hear Nobody Pray.**

Arr copyright, 1925, by Robert H. Coleman.   Arr. B. B. McKinney.

Oh, I could'nt hear no-bo-dy pray, Oh, I could'nt hear no-bo-dy pray, Oh, way down yonder by my-self;......... And I could'nt hear no-bo-dy pray.

1. Mas - sa Je - sus!...... In the val - ley, With His bur - dens And His tri - als.
2. Chil - ly wa - ters...... In the Jor - dan, Crossing o - ver In - to Ca - naan.
3. Hal - le - lu - jah!...... Trou - bles o - ver, In the king-dom With my Je - sus.

I could-'nt hear no-bod - y pray, I could'nt hear no-bo-dy pray, I could-'nt hear no-bod - y pray;

I Could'nt Hear Nobody Pray.

No. 122　　　　　　　**God Be With You.**

J. E. Rankin.　　　　Arr. copyright 1928, by Robert H. Coleman.　　W. G. Tomer.
　　　　　　　　　　　　　　　　　　　　　　　　　　　　　Arr. by B. B. McK.

1. God be with you till we meet a-gain; By His counsels guide, up-hold you, With His sheep se-cure-ly fold you; God be with you till we meet a-gain.
2. God be with you till we meet a-gain; 'Neath His wings pro-tect-ing hide you, Dai-ly man-na still pro-vide you; God be with you till we meet a-gain.
3. God be with you till we meet a-gain; When life's per-ils thick con-found you, Put His arms un-fail-ing round you; God be with you till we meet a-gain.
4. God be with you till we meet a-gain; Keep love's ban-ner float-ing o'er you; Smite death's threat'ning wave be-fore you; God be with you till we meet a-gain.

CHORUS.

Till we meet, ... till we meet,
Till we meet, till we meet,
Till we meet at Je-sus' feet; .... Till we meet ....
till we meet; Till we meet,
till we meet, God be with you till we meet a-gain.
till will meet,

No. 123 Down By The River Side.

Arr. copyright, 1932, by Robert H. Coleman.

Arr. by B. B. McKinney.

1. Going to lay down my bur-den, Down by the riv-er side, Down by the
2. Going to meet my dear Fa-ther, Down by the riv-er side, Down by the
3. Going to meet my dear moth-er, Down by the riv-er side, Down by the
4. Going to meet my dear Sav-ior, Down by the riv-er side, Down by the

riv - er side, Down by the riv - er side; Going to lay down my bur-den,
riv - er side, Down by the riv - er side; Going to meet my dear Fa-ther,
riv - er side, Down by the riv - er side; Going to meet my dear moth-er,
riv - er side, Down by the riv - er side; Going to meet my dear Sav-ior,

CHORUS.

Down by the riv - er side, To stud-y war no more. Aint a gon-na stud-y war no more, Aint a gon-na stud-y war no more, Aint a-gon-na

1. stud-y war no more, ... 2. Stud-y war no more.
   more, no more, no more,

No. 124 Going To Shout All Over God's Heaven.

Arr. copyright 1921, by Rob't H. Coleman. **Arr. by B. B. McKinney.**

1. I've got a robe, you've got a robe, All of God's children got a robe;
2. I've got a crown, you've got a crown, All of God's children got a crown;
3. I've got a shoes, you've got a shoes, All of God's children got a shoes;
4. I've got a harp, you've got a harp, All of God's children got a harp:
5. I've got a song, you've got a song, All of God's children got a song;

When I get to heav-en, goin' to put on my robe, Goin' to shout all
When I get to heav-en, goin' to put on my crown, Goin' to shout all
When I get to heav-en, goin' to put on my shoes, Goin' to walk all
When I get to heav-en, goin' to play on my harp, Goin' to play all
When I get to heav-en, goin' to sing a new song, Goin' to sing all

Chorus.

o-ver God's heav-en. Heav-en,* heav-en, Ev-'ry-bod-y talk-ing 'bout

heav'n ain't a goin' there, Heav'n, heav'n, Goin' to shout all over God's heav'n.

*Let the last syllable of heav'n be a hum.

No. 125 **Some O' These Days.**

Arr. copyright, 1905, by Robert H. Coleman.   Arr. B. B. McKinney.

1. I'm a-go-na walk on the streets of glo - ry, oh, yes,
2. I'm a-go-na shout and sing for-ev - er, oh, yes,
3. I'm a-go-na see my saint-ed moth - er, oh, yes,
4. I'm a-go-na see my bless-ed Sav - ior, oh, yes,

I'm a-go-na walk on the streets of glo-ry Some o' these days;
I'm a-go-na sing and shout for-ev-er Some o' these days;
I'm a-go-na see my saint-ed moth-er Some o' these days;
I'm a-go-na see my bless-ed Sav-ior Some o' these days;

Hal-le-lu-jah, I'm a-go-na walk on the streets of glo - ry,
Hal-le-lu-jah, I'm a-go-na sing and shout for-ev - er,
Hal-le-lu-jah, I'm a-go-na see my saint-ed moth - er,
Hal-le-lu-jah, I'm a-go-na see my bless-ed Sav - ior,

Go-na walk on the streets of glo-ry Some o' these days.
Go-na sing and shout for-ev-er Some o' these days.
Go-na see my saint-ed moth-er Some o' these days.
Go-na see my bless-ed Sav-ior Some o' these days.

No. 126 Hush! Somebody's Calling My Name.

Arr. copyright, 1928, by Robert H. Coleman.

Arr. by B. B. McKinney.

Hush! hush! somebody's calling my name; Hush! hush! somebody's calling my name; Hush! hush! some-bod-y's call-ing my name; O my Lord, O my Lord, what shall I do?

1. I'm so glad that trouble don't last always;
2. I'm so glad I got re-lig-ion in time;
3. I'm so glad my soul's got a hid-ing place;

Hal-le-lu-jah!

I'm so glad that trou-ble don't last always;
I'm so glad I got re-lig-ion in time;
I'm so glad my soul's got a hid-ing place;

ways;.......... O my Lord, O my Lord, what shall I do?
time;........... O my Lord, O my Lord, what shall I do?
place;.......... O my Lord, O my Lord, what shall I do?
O glo-ry!

No. 127 **I Know The Lord.**

Arr. copyright, 1928, by Robert H. Coleman.

Arr. by B. B. McKinney.

O I know the Lord, I know the Lord, I know the
Lord laid His hands on me.

O was-n't that a hap-py day?
Did e'er you see the light be-fore?
I'll meet you in the prom-ised land;

I know the Lord laid His hands on me.

When Je-sus washed our sins a-way,
King Je-sus preach-ing to the poor?
We'll take King Je-sus by the hand;

I know the Lord laid His hands on me.

No. 128 Swing Low.

Arr. copyright 1921, by Rob't H. Coleman. Arr. by B. B. McKinney.

Swing low, sweet char-i-ot, Com-ing for to car-ry me home; Swing low, sweet char-i-ot, Com-ing for to car-ry me home.

Hum............ hum...... Hum........ Hum..

1. I looked o-ver Jor-dan, what did I see Coming for to car-ry me home? A band of an-gels com-ing af-ter me, Com-ing for to car-ry me home.
2. If you get there be-fore I do, Coming for to car-ry me home; Tell all my friends I'm com-ing, too, Com-ing for to car-ry me home.
3. I'm some-times up, I'm some-times down, Coming for to car-ry me home; But still my soul is heav'n-ward bound, Com-ing for to car-ry me home.

.... Hum.................... Hum.. .... Hum..

No. 129 The Royal Telephone.

F. M. L.

Copyright, 1909, by F. M. Lehman. Used by permission.

F. M. Lehman.
Arr. B. B. McKinney.

1. Central's nev-er "bus-y," Al-ways on the line, You may hear from heaven Al-most an-y time.
2. There will be no charges, Tel-e-phone is free; It was built for ser-vice, Just for you and me.
3. Fail to get the an-swer, Satan's crossed your wire By some strong de-lu-sion, Or some base de-sire.
4. Car-nal com-bin-a-tions Can-not get control Of this line to glo-ry, Anchored in the soul.

'Tis a roy-al serv-ice, Free for one and all—
There will be no wait-ing On this roy-al line—
Take a-way obstructions— God is on the throne—
Storm and tri-al can-not Dis-con-nect the line

FINE. CHORUS.

When you get in trou-ble Give this roy-al line a call.
Tel-e-phone to glo-ry Al-ways an-swers just in time.
And you'll get the an-swer Thro' this roy-al tel-a-phone.
Held in con-stant keep-ing By the Fa-ther's hand di-vine.

Tel-e-phone to

D.S. We may talk to Je-sus Thro' this roy-al tel-e-phone.

glo-ry, O what joy di-vine! I can feel the cur-rent Mov-ing on the line; Built by God the Fa-ther For His loved and own—

No. 130 Walk In Jerusalem Just Like John.

Arr. copyright, 1928, by Robert H. Coleman.

Arr. by B. B. McKinney.

I want to be read-y, I want to be read-y,

I want to be read-y, To walk in Je-ru-sa-lem just like John.

1. O John, O John, now didn't you say? Walk in Je-ru-sa-lem just like John;
2. Some came crippled, and some came lame, Walk in Je-ru-sa-lem just like John;
3. Now, brother, better mind how you step on the cross, Walk in Je-ru-sa-lem just like John;
4. If you get there be-fore I do, Walk in Je-ru-sa-lem just like John;

That you'd be there on that great day, Walk in Je-ru-sa-lem just like John.
Some came walkin' in Je-sus' name, Walk in Je-ru-sa-lem just like John.
Your feet might slip and your soul get lost, Walk in Je-ru-sa-lem just like John.
Tell all my friends I'm a-coming too, Walk in Je-ru-sa-lem just like John.

No. 131 Glimbing Up Zion's Hill.

Arr. copyright, 1932, by Robert H. Coleman

Words Arr. by B. B. McK. Negro Spiritual Arr. by B. B. McKinney.

CHORUS.

I'm climbing, I'm climbing, I'm climbing, thank God, I'm climbing up Zi - on's hill;

I'm climbing, I'm climbing the pathway He trod, I'm climbing up Zion's hill.

Verse.

1. My soul is an-chored in the Lord, I'm climbing up Zi - on's hill;
2. Tho' oft - en tossed and driv'n a - bout, I'm climbing up Zi - on's hill;
3. I know my name is writ - ten there, I'm climbing up Zi - on's hill;
4. By faith I view that gold - en shore, I'm climbing up Zi - on's hill;

I'm ful - ly trust - ing in His word, I'm climbing up Zi - on's hill.
I'll trust in Him and nev - er doubt, I'm climbing up Zi - on's hill.
I'll soon be free from ev - 'ry care, I'm climbing up Zi - on's hill.
I'm go - ing there to die no more, I'm climbing up Zi - on's hill

No. 132　　　　　　　Auld Lang Syne.

Arr. copyright, 1928, by Robert H. Coleman.　　Arr. B. B. McKinney.

1. Should auld acquaintance be for-got, And nev-er brought to mind?
2. We twa hae run a-boot the braes, And pu'd the gow-ans fine;
3. We twa hae sport-ed i' the burn Frae morn-in' sun till dine,
4. And here's a hand, my trust-y frien', And gie's a hand o' thine;

Should auld ac-quaint-ance be for-got, And days of auld lang syne?
But we've wandered mony a wea-ry foot, Sin' auld lang syne.
But seas be-tween us braid hae roared Sin' auld lang syne.
We'll tak' a cup o' kind-ness yet, For auld lang syne.

CHORUS.

For auld lang syne, my dear, For auld lang syne;

We'll tak' a cup o' kind-ness yet, For auld lang syne.

No. 133   **Four And Twenty Elders.**

Arr. copyright, 1925, by Robert H. Coleman.

Arr. B. B. McKinney.

1. See four and twen-ty el-ders on their knees,........
2. They're bow-ing round the al-ter on their knees,........
3. See Dan-iel in den of li-ons on his knees,........
4. We'll praise our Lord to-geth-er on our knees,........

See four and twen-ty el-ders on their knees.
They're bow-ing round the al-ter on their knees.
See Dan-iel in den of li-ons on his knees.
We'll praise our Lord to-geth-er on our knees.

CHORUS.

And we'll all rise to-geth-er and face the ris-ing sun,

Oh, Lord, have mer-cy, if you please....
oh, Lord, if you please.

No. 134. Standing In The Need Of Prayer.

PLANTATION MELODY.

Arr. copyright 1921, by Rob't H. Coleman.   Arr. by B. B. McKinney.

Plaintive.

1. Not my brother, nor my sis-ter, but it's me, O Lord, Standing in the need of pray'r; Not my brother, nor my sis-ter, but it's me, O Lord,
2. Not my fa-ther, nor my moth-er, but it's me, O Lord, Standing in the need of pray'r; Not my fa-ther, nor my moth-er, but it's me, O Lord,
3. Not the dea-con, nor my pas-tor, but it's me, O Lord, Standing in the need of pray'r; Not the dea-con, nor my pas-tor, but it's me, O Lord,

CHORUS.

Standing in the need of pray'r. It's me, (it's me,) it's me, O Lord,

Standing in the need of pray'r; It's me, (it's me,) it's me, O Lord,

CODA. *rit.*

Standing in the need of pray'r. Standing in the need of pray'r.

No. 135   Old Black Joe.

S. F. C.   Stephen C. Foster.

1. Gone are the days when my heart was young and gay; Gone are my friends from the cot-ton fields a-way; Gone from the earth to a bet-ter land I know, I hear their gen-tle voi-ces call-ing,
2. Why do I weep when my heart should feel no pain? Why do I sigh that my friends come not a-gain? Griev-ing for forms now de-part-ed long a-go, I hear their gen-tle voi-ces call-ing,
3. Where are the hearts once so hap-py and so free? The children so dear that I held up-on my knee? Gone to the shore where my soul has longed to go, I hear their gen-tle voi-ces call-ing,

CHORUS.

"Old Black Joe!" I'm com-ing, I'm com-ing, For my head is bend-ing low; I hear their gen-tle voi-ces call-ing, "Old Black Joe!"
For my head is bending low;

SM-5

No. 136 Steal Away.

Arr. copyright, 1932, by Robert H. Coleman. **Arr. B. B. McKinney.**

Steal a-way to Je-sus, Steal a-way
Steal a-way to Je-sus, Steal a-way
Steal a-way to Je-sus, Steal a-way

Steal a-way home, I have not long to stay here.
Steal a-way home,

Faster.

1. My Lord calls me, He calls me by the thun-der,
2. Green trees are bend-ing, Poor sin-ners stand a trem-bling,
3. My Lord calls me, He calls me by the light-ning,
4. Tombstones are burst-ing, Poor sin-ners stand a trem-bling,

The trumpet sounds it in my soul, I have not long to stay here.

No. 137 In My Heart.

Old melody.

With feeling.

1. Lord, I want to be a Christian In my heart, in my heart, Lord, I
2. Lord, I want to be more humble In my heart, in my heart, Lord, I
3. Lord, I want to be like Je-sus In my heart, in my heart, Lord, I

In My Heart.

CHORUS.

want to be a Christian In my heart. In my heart,........ in my
want to be more humble In my heart.
want to be like Jesus In my heart. In my heart,

heart,.......... Lord, I want to be a Christian in my heart.
Lord, I want to be more hum-ble in my heart.
in my heart, Lord, I want to be like Je-sus in my heart.

No. 138   "Good Night, Ladies."

f Sostenuto.

1. Good-night, la - dies! good-night, la - dies! Good-night,
2. Fare-well, la - dies! fare-well, la - dies! Fare - well,
3. Sweet dreams, la - dies! sweet dreams, la - dies! Sweet dreams,

Allegro.

la - dies! We're going to leave you now. Mer-ri-ly we roll a-long,

Repeat pp

roll a-long, roll a-long, Mer-ri-ly we roll a-long, O'er the dark blue sea.

No. 139   Life's Railway To Heaven.
Male Quartet arrangement—Copyright, 1924, by Charlie D. Tillman.

M. E. Abbey.   Charlie D. Tillman.

1. Life is like a moun-tain rail-road, With an en-gi-neer that's brave;
2. You will roll up grades of tri - al; You will cross the bridge of strife;
3. You will oft - en find ob-struc-tions; Look for storms of wind and rain;
4. As you roll a-cross the tres-tle, Spanning Jor-dan's swell-ing tide;

We must make the run suc-cess-ful From the cra - dle to the grave:
See that Christ is your con-duc-tor On this light'ning train of life;
On a fill, or curve, or tres-tle, They will al - most ditch your train:
You be-hold the Un - ion De - pot In - to which your train will glide:

Watch the curves, the fills, the tun - nels; Nev - er fal - ter, nev - er quail;
Al - ways mind - ful of ob-struc-tion, Do your du - ty, nev - er fail;
Put your trust a - lone in Je - sus; Nev - er fal - ter, nev - er fail;
There you'll meet the Su-perin-tend'-ant, God, the Fa - ther, God, the Son;

Keep your hand up - on the throt-tle, And your eye up - on the rail.
Keep your hand up - on the throt-tle, And your eye up - on the rail.
Keep your hand up - on the throt-tle, And your eye up - on the rail.
With the heart - y joy - ous plaud-it, "Wea - ry pil - grim, wel-come home."

Life's Railway To Heaven.

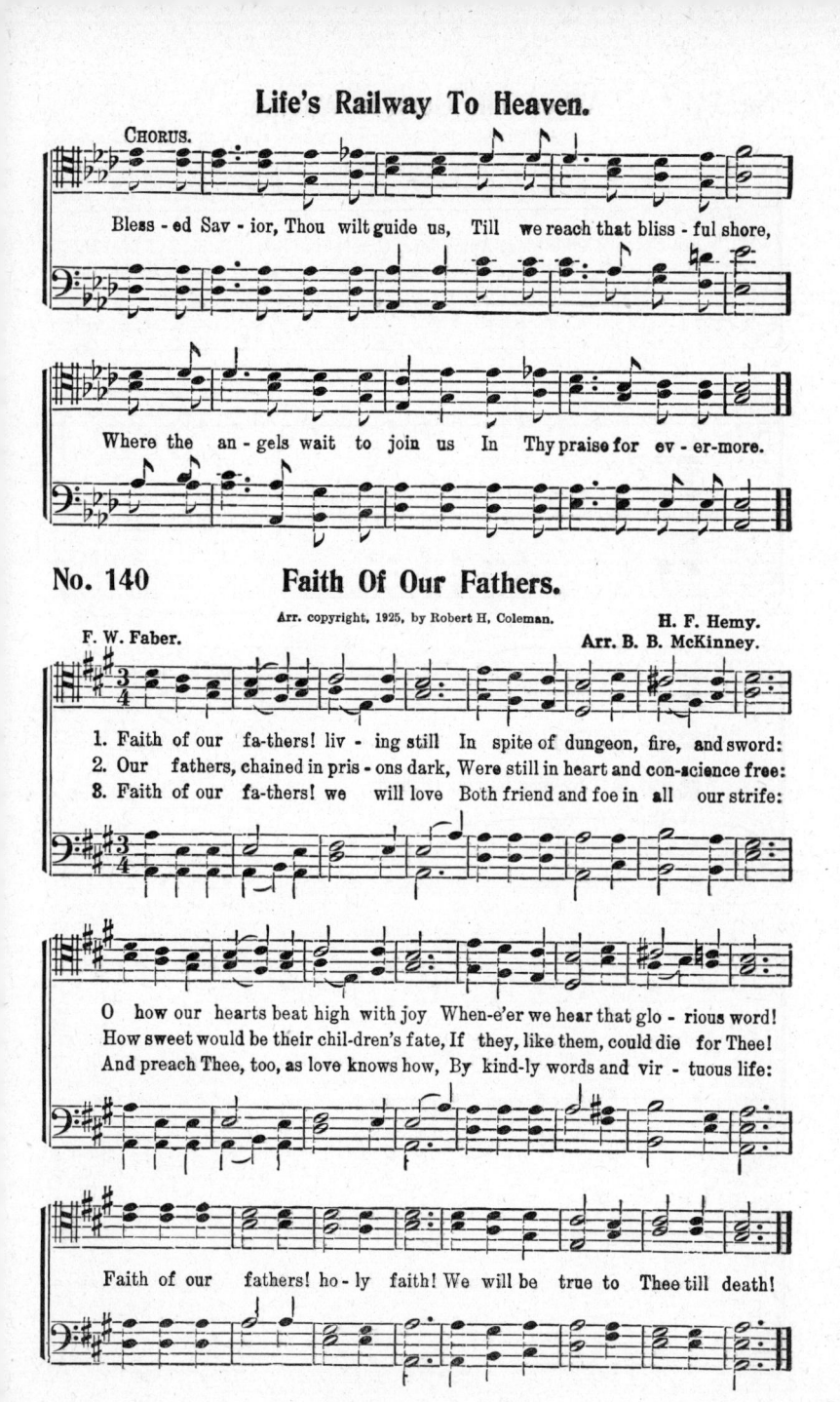

CHORUS.

Bless-ed Sav-ior, Thou wilt guide us, Till we reach that bliss-ful shore,
Where the an-gels wait to join us In Thy praise for ev-er-more.

No. 140 Faith Of Our Fathers.

Arr. copyright, 1925, by Robert H, Coleman.

F. W. Faber.
H. F. Hemy.
Arr. B. B. McKinney.

1. Faith of our fa-thers! liv-ing still In spite of dungeon, fire, and sword:
2. Our fathers, chained in pris-ons dark, Were still in heart and con-science free:
3. Faith of our fa-thers! we will love Both friend and foe in all our strife:

O how our hearts beat high with joy When-e'er we hear that glo-rious word!
How sweet would be their chil-dren's fate, If they, like them, could die for Thee!
And preach Thee, too, as love knows how, By kind-ly words and vir-tuous life:

Faith of our fathers! ho-ly faith! We will be true to Thee till death!

No. 141 — When The Corn Is Waving.

C. Blamphin.   Arr. copyright, 1932, by Robert H. Coleman.   Arr. B. B. McKinney.

1. When the corn is wav-ing, Annie dear, O meet me by the stile, I hear thy gen-tle voice a-gain, And greet thy winning smile; The moon will be at full, love, The stars will bright-ly gleam, Oh come, my queen of night, love, Oh come, my queen And grace the beauteous scene.

2. When the corn is wav-ing, Annie dear, Our tales of love we'll tell, Beside the gen-tle flowing stream, That both our hearts know well, Where wild flow'rs in their beau-ty, Will scent the eve-ning breeze, Oh haste, the stars are peep-ing, Oh haste, the stars The moon's be-hind the trees.

REFRAIN.

When the corn is wav-ing; An-nie dear, Oh meet me by the stile, I hear thy gentle voice again, And greet thy winning smile.

No. 142 **Carry Me Back to Old Virginny.**

Arr. Copyright, 1921, by Rob't H. Coleman.

James Black. Arr. by B. B. McKinney.

1. Car-ry me back to old Vir-gin-ny, There's where the cot-ton and the corn and ta-toes grow, There's where the birds warble sweet in the springtime, There's where this old darkey's heart am long to go; There's where I la-bored so hard for old Mas-sa, Day af-ter day in the fields of yel-low corn, No place on earth do I love more sin-cere-ly, Than old Vir-gin-ny the state where I was born.

2. Car-ry me back to old Vir-gin-ny, There let me live un-til I with-er and de-cay, Down by the old dismal swamp have I wan-dered, There's where this old darkey's life will pass a-way; Mas-sa and Mis-sis have long gone be-fore me, Soon we will meet on that bright and golden shore, There we'll be hap-py and free from all sor-row, There's where we'll meet and we'll nev-er part no more.

CHORUS.

D. C.—Car-ry me back to old Vir-gin-ny, There's where the cot-ton and the corn and ta-toes grow, There's where the birds warble sweet in the springtime, There's where this old darkey's heart am long to go.

FINE.

D. C. for Chorus.

No. 143 **Crossing The Bar.**

Alfred Tennyson.
Copyright, 1928, by Robert H. Coleman.
International copyright secured.
B. B. McKinney.

1. Sun-set and eve-ning star, And one clear call for me; And may there be no moan-ing of the bar When I put out to sea,... When I put out to sea. But such a tide as mov-ing seems a-sleep, To pull for sound and foam, When that which drew from out the boundless deep, Turns a-gain home; Turns a-gain home.

2. Twi-light and eve-ning bell, And af-ter that the dark, And may there be no sad-ness of fare-well When I, when I em-bark,... When I, when I em-bark. For tho' from out our bourne of time and space, The flood may bear me far, I know I'll see my Pi-lot face to face, When I have crossed the bar; I have crossed the bar.

No. 144 Rocked In The Cradle Of The Deep.

Emma Willard. Arr. copyright, 1928, by Robert H. Coleman. Arr. by B. B. McKinney.

1. Rock'd in the cra-dle of the deep, I lay me down in peace to sleep;
2. And such the trust that still were mine, Tho' stormy winds swept o'er the brine,

Se-cure I rest up-on the wave, For Thou, oh, Lord, hast pow'r to save.
Or tho' the tempest fie - ry breath Rous'd me from sleep to wreck and death.

I know Thou wilt not slight my call, For Thou dost mark the sparrow's fall;
In ocean cave still safe with Thee, The germ of im-mor-tal-i-ty;

REFRAIN.

And calm and peaceful is my sleep, Rock'd in the cra-dle of the deep.

rit.

And calm and peaceful is my sleep, Rock'd in the cra-dle of the deep.

No. 145 My Old Kentucky Home.

S. C. F. Stephen C. Foster.

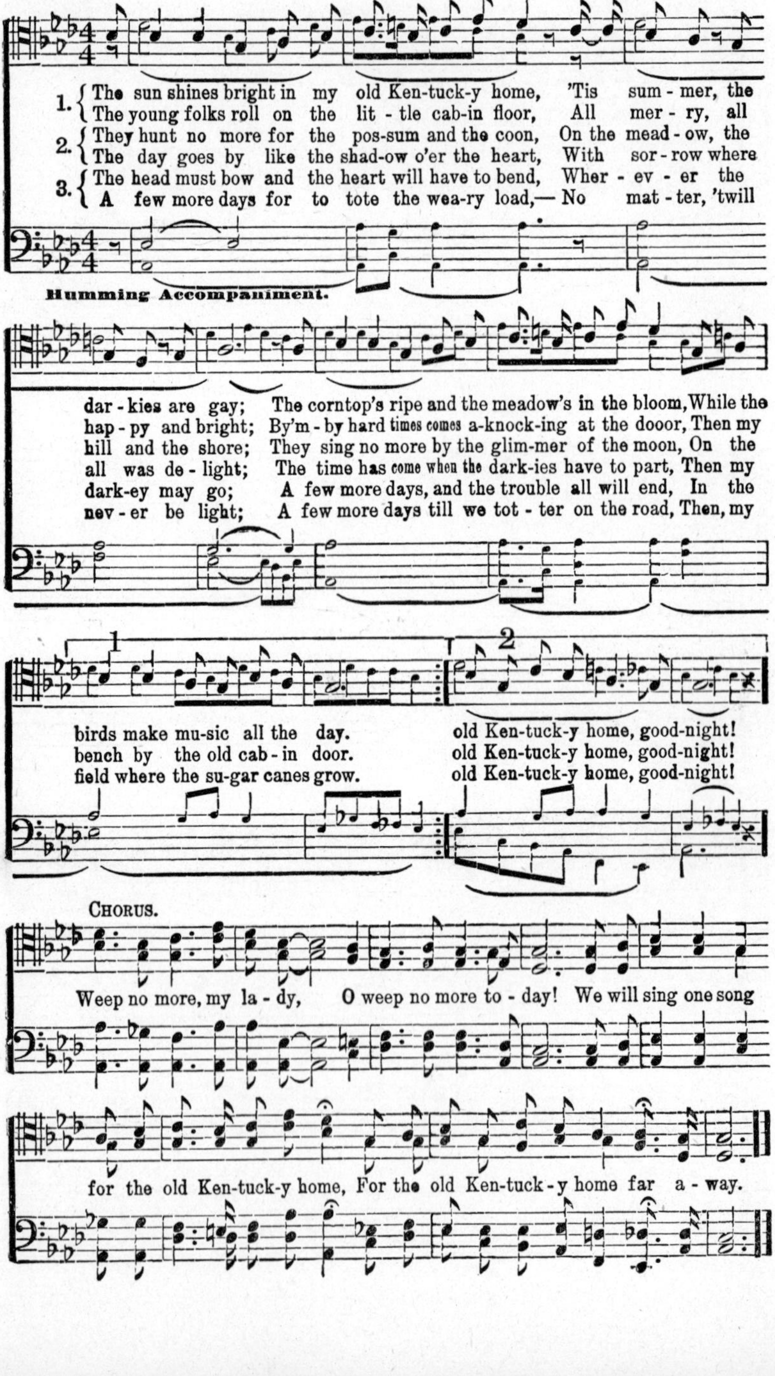

No. 146   Old Folks At Home.

S. C. F.   SWANEE RIVER.   Stephen C. Foster.

1. { Way down up-on the Swa-nee Riv-er Far, far a-way;
    All up and down de whole cre-a-tion, Sad-ly I roam,

2. { All roun' de lit-tle farm I wan-dered, When I was young;
    When I was play-ing with my broth-er, Hap-py was I:

3. { One lit-tle hut a-mong de bush-es, One that I love;
    When will I see de bees a hum-ming, All roun' de comb?

Humming accompaniment.

Dere's wha my heart is turn-ing ev-er, Dere's wha de old folks stay.
Still long-ing for de old plan-ta-tion, And for de old folks at home.

Den ma-ny hap-py days I squandered, Ma-ny de songs I sung.
Oh! take me to my kind old moth-er, There let me live and die.

Still sad-ly to my mem-'ry rush-es, No mat-ter where I roam.
When will I hear de ban-jo tum-ming, Down in my good old home.

Chorus.

All de world is sad and drear-y, Ev-'ry-where I roam;

Oh! dark-ies how my heart grows weary, Far from de old folks at home.

No. 147 **The Star-Spangled Banner.**

Arr. copyright, 1928, by Robert H. Coleman.

F. S. Key.   Arr. by B. B. McKinney.

1. Oh, say, can you see, by the dawn's early light, What so proudly we hailed at the twi-light's last gleaming, Whose broad stripes and bright stars, thro' the per-il-ous fight, O'er the ramparts we watched, were so gal-lant-ly streaming? And the rockets' red glare, the bombs bursting in air, Gave proof thro' the
2. On the shore dimly seen thro' the mists of the deep, Where the foes haughty host in dread si-lence re-pos-es, What is that which the breeze, o'er the tow-er-ing steep, As it fit-ful-ly blows, half conceals, half dis-clos-es? Now it catches the gleam of the morning's first beam, In full glo-ry re-
3. And where is that band who so vaunt-ing-ly swore, That the hav-oc of war and the bat-tle's con-fu-sion, A home and a coun-try should leave us no more? Their blood has washed out their foul footsteps pol-lu-tion. No ref-uge could save the hire-ling and slave From the ter-ror of
4. Oh, thus be it ev-er when free-men shall stand Between their loved home and wild war's des-o-la-tion; Blest with vict'ry and peace, may the heav'n-res-cued land Praise the Pow'r that hath made and preserved us a na-tion! Then conquer we must, when our cause it is just, And this be our

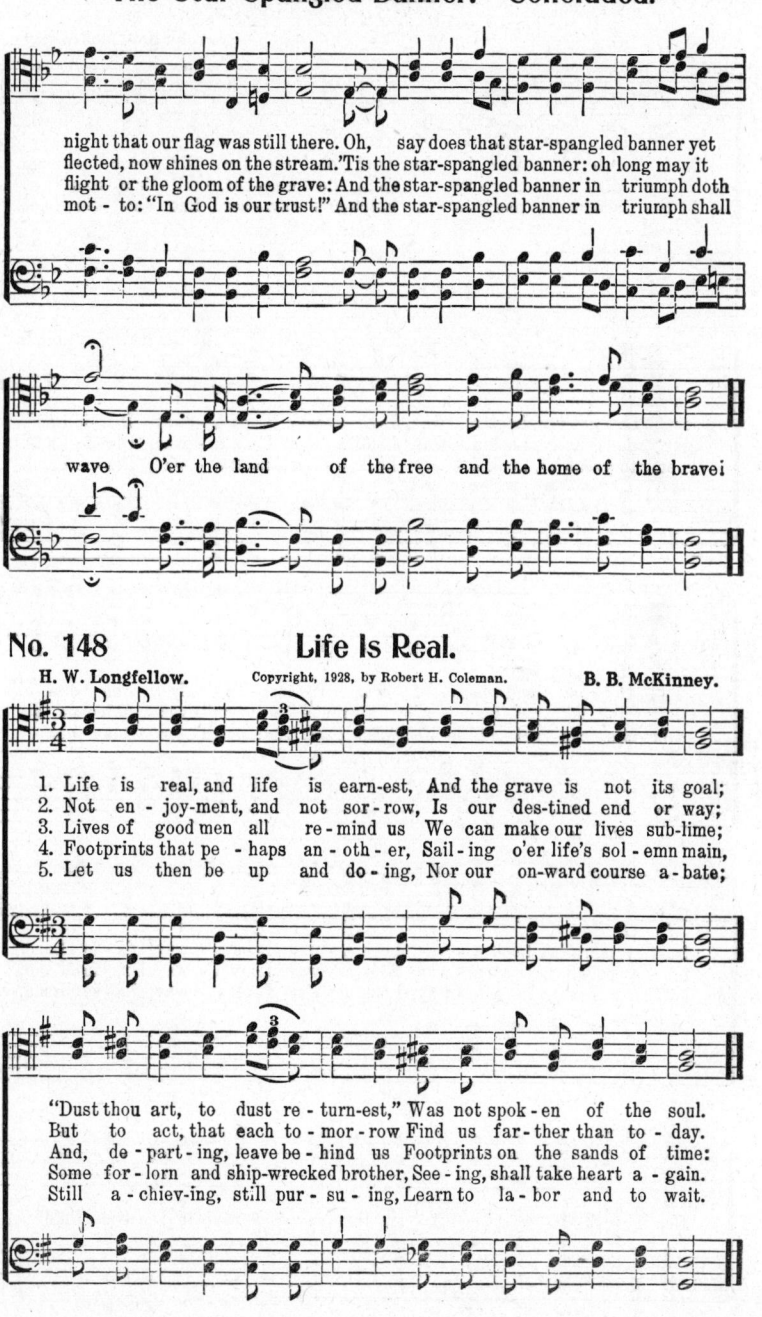

The Star-Spangled Banner. Concluded.

night that our flag was still there. Oh, say does that star-spangled banner yet
flected, now shines on the stream.'Tis the star-spangled banner: oh long may it
flight or the gloom of the grave: And the star-spangled banner in triumph doth
mot - to: "In God is our trust!" And the star-spangled banner in triumph shall

wave O'er the land of the free and the home of the brave!

No. 148   Life Is Real.

H. W. Longfellow.   Copyright, 1928, by Robert H. Coleman.   B. B. McKinney.

1. Life is real, and life is earn-est, And the grave is not its goal;
2. Not en - joy-ment, and not sor-row, Is our des-tined end or way;
3. Lives of good men all re-mind us We can make our lives sub-lime;
4. Footprints that pe - haps an - oth - er, Sail-ing o'er life's sol - emn main,
5. Let us then be up and do - ing, Nor our on-ward course a - bate;

"Dust thou art, to dust re - turn-est," Was not spok - en of the soul.
But to act, that each to - mor - row Find us far - ther than to - day.
And, de - part - ing, leave be - hind us Footprints on the sands of time:
Some for - lorn and ship-wrecked brother, See - ing, shall take heart a - gain.
Still a - chiev-ing, still pur - su - ing, Learn to la - bor and to wait.

No. 149 **Dixie Land.**

Arr. copyright, 1928, by Robert H. Coleman.

Arr. by B. B. McKinney.

1. I wish I was in de land ob cot-ton, Old times dar am not for-got-ten, Look a-way, Look a-way, Look a-way, Dix-ie Land. In Dix-ie land where I was born in, Ear-ly on one frost-y morn-in', Look a-way, Look a-way, Look a-way, Dix-ie Land.

2. Old Mis-sus mar-ry Will, de wea-ber, Wil-lium was a gay de-ceab-er, Look a-way, Look a-way, Look a-way, Dix-ie Land. But when he put his arm a-round 'er He smiled as fierce as a for-ty pounder, Look a-way, Look a-way, Look a-way, Dix-ie Land.

3. His face was sharp as a butch-er's clea-ber, But dat did not seem to greab'er, Look a-way, Look a-way, Look a-way, Dix-ie Land. Old Mis-sus act-ed de fool-ish part, And died for a man dat broke her heart, Look a-way, Look a-way, Look a-way, Dix-ie Land.

CHORUS.

Den I wish I was in Dix-ie, Hoo-ray, hoo-ray! In Dix-ie land I'll

Dixie Land. Concluded.

take my stand, To lib and die in Dix-ie; A-way, A-way, A-way down south in Dix-ie; A-way, A-way, A-way down south in Dix-ie.

No. 150　　　Tramp! Tramp! Tramp!

Arr. copyright, 1928, by Robert H. Coleman.

Geo. F. Root.
B. B. McK.

Tramp, tramp, tramp, the boys are march-ing, Cheer up com-rades
marching on, oh,
they will come, And be-neath the star-ry flag, We will
will come,
breathe the air a-gain, Of the free-land in our own be-lov-ed home.

No. 151. Home, Sweet Home.

Payne. Arr. copyright, 1928, by Robert H. Coleman. Arr. by B. B. McKinney.

1. 'Mid pleas-ures and pal-a-ces though we may roam,
2. An ex-ile from home, splen-dor daz-zles in vain—
3. To us, in de-spite of the ab-sence of years

Be it ev-er so hum-ble there's no place like home!
O give me my low-ly thatch'd cot-age a-gain;
How sweet— the re-mem-brance of home still ap-pears;

A charm from the skies seems to hal-low us there.
The birds sing-ing gai-ly that come at my call,
From al-lur-ments a-broad which but flat-ter the eye,

Which seek thro' the world, is ne'er met with elsewhere.
Give me these and peace of mind dear-er than all.
The un-sat-is-fied heart turns and says with a sigh,—

REFRAIN.

Home, home sweet, sweet home! There's no place like home, There's no place like home!

SOLOS, DUETS AND OTHER SPECIALS

152. I Walk With the King.

James Rowe.
COPYRIGHT, 1913, BY HOMER A. RODEHEAVER.
INTERNATIONAL COPYRIGHT SECURED.
B. D. Ackley.

1. In sor-row I wan-dered, my spir-it op-prest, But now I am hap-py—se-cure-ly I rest; From morn-ing till eve-ning glad car-ols I sing, And this is the rea-son—I walk with the King.
2. For years in the fet-ters of sin I was bound, The world could not help me—no com-fort I found; But now like the birds and the sun-beams of Spring, I'm free and re-joic-ing—I walk with the King.
3. O soul near de-spair in the low-lands of strife, Look up and let Je-sus come in-to your life; The joy of sal-va-tion to you He would bring—Come in-to the sun-light and walk with the King.

REFRAIN.

I walk with the King, hal-le-lu-jah! I walk with the King, praise His name!
No lon-ger I roam, my soul fac-es home, I walk and I talk with the King.

153 My Pilot Will Land the Boat.

B. B. McK.
COPYRIGHT, 1932, BY ROBERT H. COLEMAN.
INTERNATIONAL COPYRIGHT SECURED.
B. B. McKinney.

BASS SOLO.

1. Tho' the tides may sweep O'er the an-gry deep, My Pi-lot will land the boat;
2. Tho' the way is dim, Put your trust in Him, My Pi-lot will land the boat;
3. Thro' the stormy night Shines the beacon light, My Pi-lot will land the boat;

Tho' we face the gales He has set the sails, My Pi-lot will land the boat.
O'er the waves that roll He has full con-trol, My Pi-lot will land the boat.
Thro' the harbor gate, Where the loved ones wait, My Pi-lot will land the boat.

CHORUS.

My Pi-lot will land the boat, . . My Pi-lot will land the boat,
the boat, the boat,

Tho' the lightnings flash And the mad waves clash, My Pi-lot will land the boat.

154 He Loves Me.

(WHY I SING.)

A. H. A. COPYRIGHT, 1930, BY ROBERT H. COLEMAN. A. H. Ackley.
INTERNATIONAL COPYRIGHT SECURED.

1. My con-fi-dence in Je-sus grows stronger ev-'ry day, His grace I find suf-fi-cient to keep me in life's way; When I am sad and lone-ly He is a friend in-deed; He gives me grace and com-fort in ev-'ry time of need.
2. His love for me is more than a moth-er's for her child, A love that sought and found me up-on the des-ert wild; His hand of mer-cy led me back to my Father's home; I know that He will love me no mat-ter what may come.
3. When I am sore-ly tempt-ed to mur-mur and complain; The way grows dark be-fore me and life is filled with pain; The tho't of all His good-ness re-stores my troubled mind; No mat-ter what be-falls me I know that God is kind.

CHORUS

He loves me, He's liv-ing in my heart; He loves me, He nev-er will de-part; He loves me, He died for me on Cal-va-ry, And that is why I sing He loves me.

155 There Are No Shadows in the Valley.

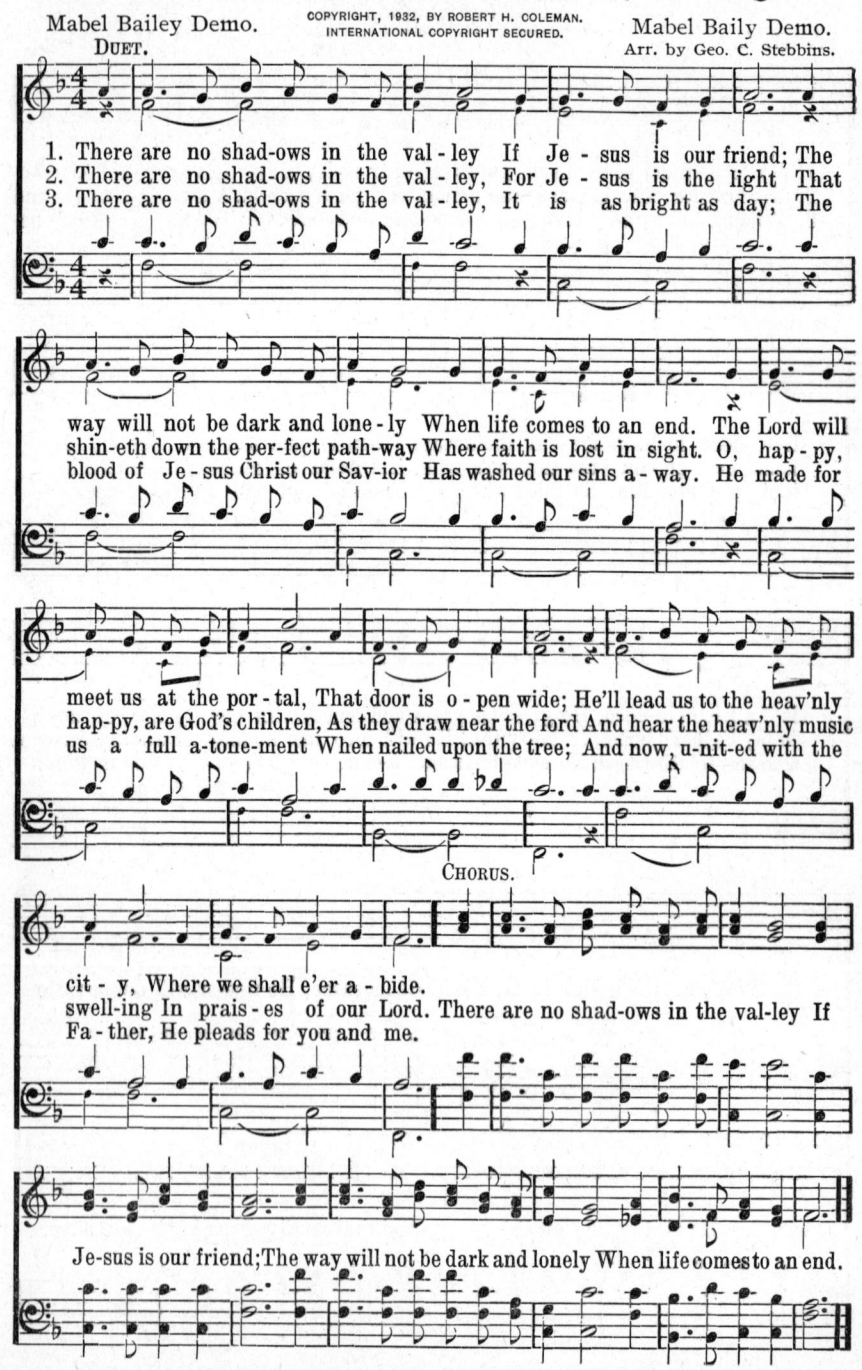

Mabel Bailey Demo.
DUET.
COPYRIGHT, 1932, BY ROBERT H. COLEMAN.
INTERNATIONAL COPYRIGHT SECURED.
Mabel Baily Demo.
Arr. by Geo. C. Stebbins.

1. There are no shad-ows in the val-ley If Je-sus is our friend; The way will not be dark and lone-ly When life comes to an end. The Lord will meet us at the por-tal, That door is o-pen wide; He'll lead us to the heav'nly cit-y, Where we shall e'er a-bide.

2. There are no shad-ows in the val-ley, For Je-sus is the light That shin-eth down the per-fect path-way Where faith is lost in sight. O, hap-py, hap-py, are God's children, As they draw near the ford And hear the heav'nly music swell-ing In prais-es of our Lord.

3. There are no shad-ows in the val-ley, It is as bright as day; The blood of Je-sus Christ our Sav-ior Has washed our sins a-way. He made for us a full a-tone-ment When nailed upon the tree; And now, u-nit-ed with the Fa-ther, He pleads for you and me.

CHORUS.

There are no shad-ows in the val-ley If Je-sus is our friend; The way will not be dark and lonely When life comes to an end.

156. Because.

A. H. A.
Rev. A. H. Ackley.

COPYRIGHT, 1931, BY ROBERT H. COLEMAN.
INTERNATIONAL COPYRIGHT SECURED.

1. How could Christ love such a world, Dark with sin and woe,
2. Loves me in my sin-ful plight, With a love that's sad;
3. O Tran-scend-ent Love Di-vine, By whose grace we live,

In-to con-dem-na-tion hurled By the might-y foe? He could love the
Loves me when my heart is right, With a love that's glad; Loves me when my
Long as breathing shall be mine, All to Him I give; All to Him who

u-ni-verse, True to His com-mand, But His love for one per-verse,
love grows cold, Dead to His dear claim; Loves me when my lips with-hold
loved me so, Why, I can-not tell; 'Tis e-nough for me to know

I could nev-er un-der-stand. He who dared for man to die,
Prais-es to His Ho-ly Name. He who dared for man to die,
He loves me, and all is well. He who dared for man to die,

On the cross that draws, Loves me, tho' I know not why, Loves me just because.

157 God's To-morrow.

A. H. A.
COPYRIGHT, 1928, BY HOMER A. RODEHEAVER.
INTERNATIONAL COPYRIGHT SECURED.
A. H. Ackley.

Andante

1. God's to-mor-row is a day of glad-ness, And its joys shall nev-er fade:
2. God's to-mor-row is a day of greet-ing: We shall see the Sav-ior's face;
3. God's to-mor-row is a day of glo-ry: We shall wear the crown of life;

No more weep-ing, no more sense of sad-ness, No more foes to make a-fraid.
And our long-ing hearts a-wait the meet-ing In that ho-ly, hap-py place.
Sing thro' countless years love's old, old sto-ry, Free for-ev-er from all strife.

Refrain

God's to-mor-row, God's to-mor-row, Ev-'ry cloud will pass a-way At the dawn-ing of that day; God's to-mor-row, No more sor-row, For I know that God's to-mor-row Will be bright-er than to-day!

158 Sunrise.

W. C. Poole.
B. D. Ackley.

COPYRIGHT, 1924, BY HALL-MACK CO.
INTERNATIONAL COPYRIGHT SECURED.

1. When I shall come to the end of my way, When I shall rest at the close of life's day, When "Welcome home" I shall hear Jesus say, O that will be sun-rise for me.
2. When in His beau-ty I see the great King, Join with the ransomed His prais-es to sing, When I shall join them my trib-ute to bring, O that will be sun-rise for me.
3. When life is o-ver and day-light is passed, In heav-en's har-bor my an-chor is cast, When I see Je-sus my Sav-ior at last, O that will be sun-rise for me.

Chorus

Sun-rise to-mor-row, sun-rise to-mor-row, Sun-rise in glo-ry is wait-ing for me; Sun-rise to-mor-row, sun-rise to-mor-row, Sun-rise with Je-sus for e-ter-ni-ty.

159 'Neath The Old Olive Trees.

B. B. McK.
Duet. Slowly.

COPYRIGHT, 1929, BY ROBERT H. COLEMAN.
INTERNATIONAL COPYRIGHT SECURED

B. B. McKinney.

1. 'Neath the stars of the night, Walked the Savior of light, In the gar-den of dew-lad-ened breeze; Where no light could be found, Je-sus knelt on the ground, There He prayed 'neath the old ol-ive trees.
2. All the sin of the world On the Sav-ior was hurled, As He knelt in the gar-den a-lone; Hear His soul-burdened plea, Let this cup pass from me, "E-ven so, not my will, Thine be done."
3. May my song ev-er be Of the love proffered me, By my Lord all a-lone on His knees: Praise His won-der-ful name, He who bore all my blame, As He knelt 'neath the old ol-ive trees.'

CHORUS.

'Neath the old ol-ive trees, 'Neath the old ol-ive trees, Went the Sav-ior a-lone on His knees, "Not my will, Thine be done," cried the Father's own Son, As He knelt 'neath the old ol-ive trees.

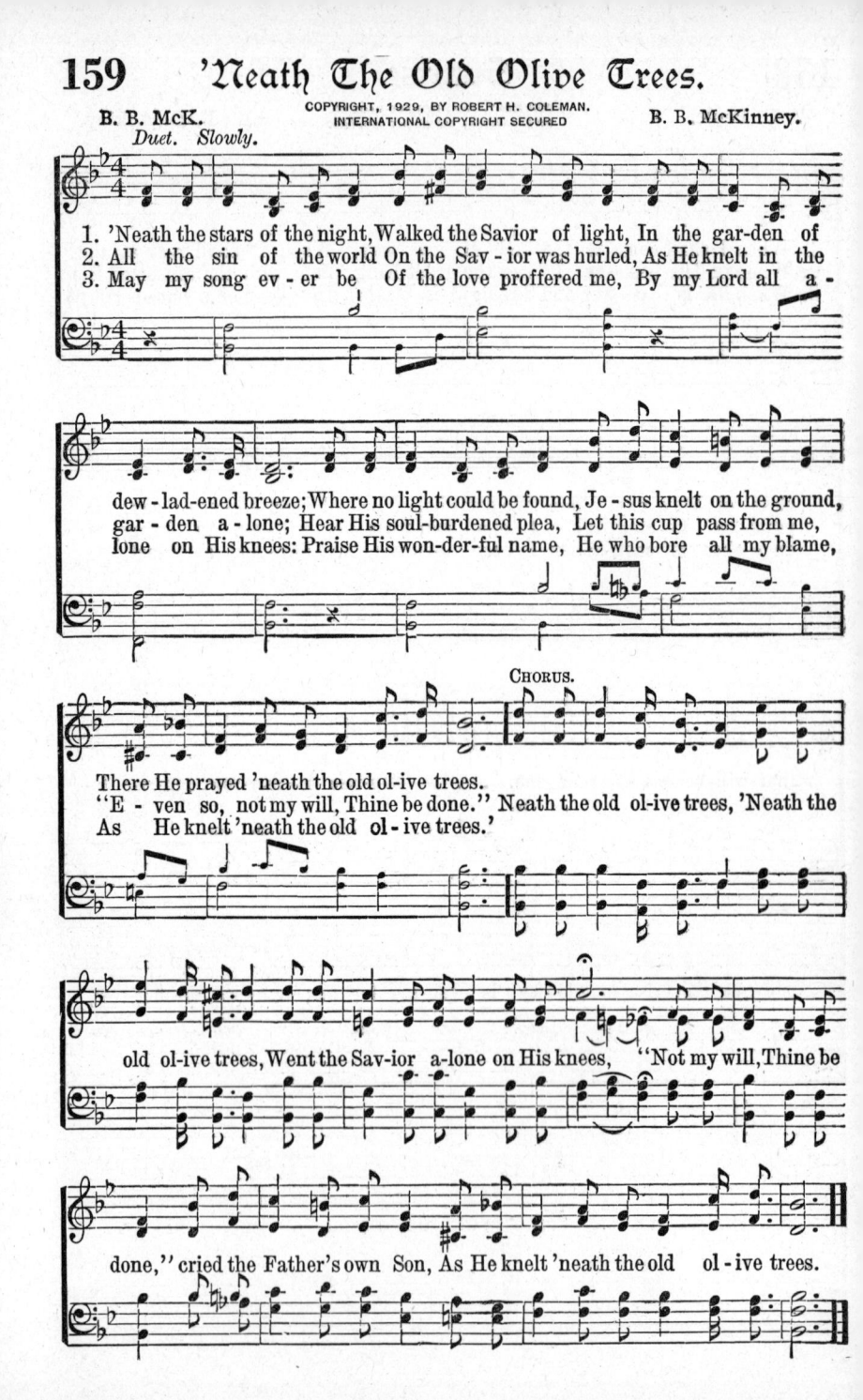

160 This Savior of Mine.

E. L.
COPYRIGHT, 1932, BY ROBERT H. COLEMAN.
INTERNATIONAL COPYRIGHT SECURED.
Evangeline Lillenas.

1. Storm clouds were rolling, my soul in de-spair, Friendships were bro-ken, but none seemed to care; Soon came a rift in the dark clouds a-bove, Je-sus re-vealed in His won-der-ful love.
2. Thus like the Sav-ior on blue Gal-i-lee, Who trod the waves of life's prob-lems for me; Bid-ding the tem-pest and waves to be still, So I have yield-ed my all to His will.
3. Skies now are bright-er, my life full of joys; Sin has de-part-ed, I'm done with earth's toys; Deep is the peace I can feel in my heart, Je-sus has made all the dis-cords de-part.

Chorus.

Oh, how I love this Sav-ior of mine, And this I know, His love is di-vine. Faith-ful I'll serve Him thro' shade or thro' shine, Oh, how I love Him, this Sav-ior of mine.

161 Leave It There.

COPYRIGHT, 1916, BY C. ALBERT TINDLEY.

Words and Music by C. Albert Tindley. Arr. by Chas. A. Tindley, Jr.

Moderato.

1. If the world from you with-hold of its sil-ver and its gold, And you
2. If your bod-y suf-fers pain, and your health you can't re-gain, And your
3. When your youthful days are gone, and old age is steal-ing on, And your

have to get a-long with mea-ger fare, Just re-mem-ber, in His word, how He
soul is al-most sink-ing in de-spair, Je-sus knows the pain you feel, He can
bod-y bends beneath the weight of care, He will nev-er leave you then, He'll go

Fine.

feeds the lit-tle bird; Take your bur-den to the Lord and leave it there.
save and He can heal; Take your bur-den to the Lord and leave it there.
with you to the end; Take your bur-den to the Lord and leave it there.

D. S.—Take your bur-den to the Lord and leave it there.

CHORUS.

Leave it there, ... leave it there, ... Take your burden to the Lord and leave it
Leave it there, leave it there,

D. S.

there; ...... If you trust and nev-er doubt, He will sure-ly bring you out;
leave it there;

162 'Twill Not Be Long.

Mrs. C. D. Martin.
COPYRIGHT, 1930, BY ROBERT H. COLEMAN.
INTERNATIONAL COPYRIGHT SECURED.
W. Stillman Martin.

DUET

1. 'Twill not be long—the burdens now we car-ry Will be laid down, and our dear Lord we'll meet; The gates of Day for us will soon be o-pened, Our jour-ney here . . . . we'll soon com-plete.
2. 'Twill not be long—the time is swift-ly pass-ing, One mo-ment here, the next with Christ our Lord; Some bus-y day our lis-t'ning ear will welcome The ho-ly sound— . . . the trump of God.
3. 'Twill not be long, but while we're watching, waiting, We'll journey on with an un-slack-ened pace; We'll keep the faith, we'll fight to win the bat-tle, And to the end . . . . we'll run the race.

CHORUS

'Twill not be long, each day brings glory near-er, 'Twill not be long that we can la-bor here; . . . . So la-bor on, be found a faith-ful serv-ant, The crowning Day is drawing nigh.

163 In the Palace of God's Love.

Dedicated to Mr. and Mrs. W. G. Taylor, Pacific Garden Mission, Chicago, Ill.

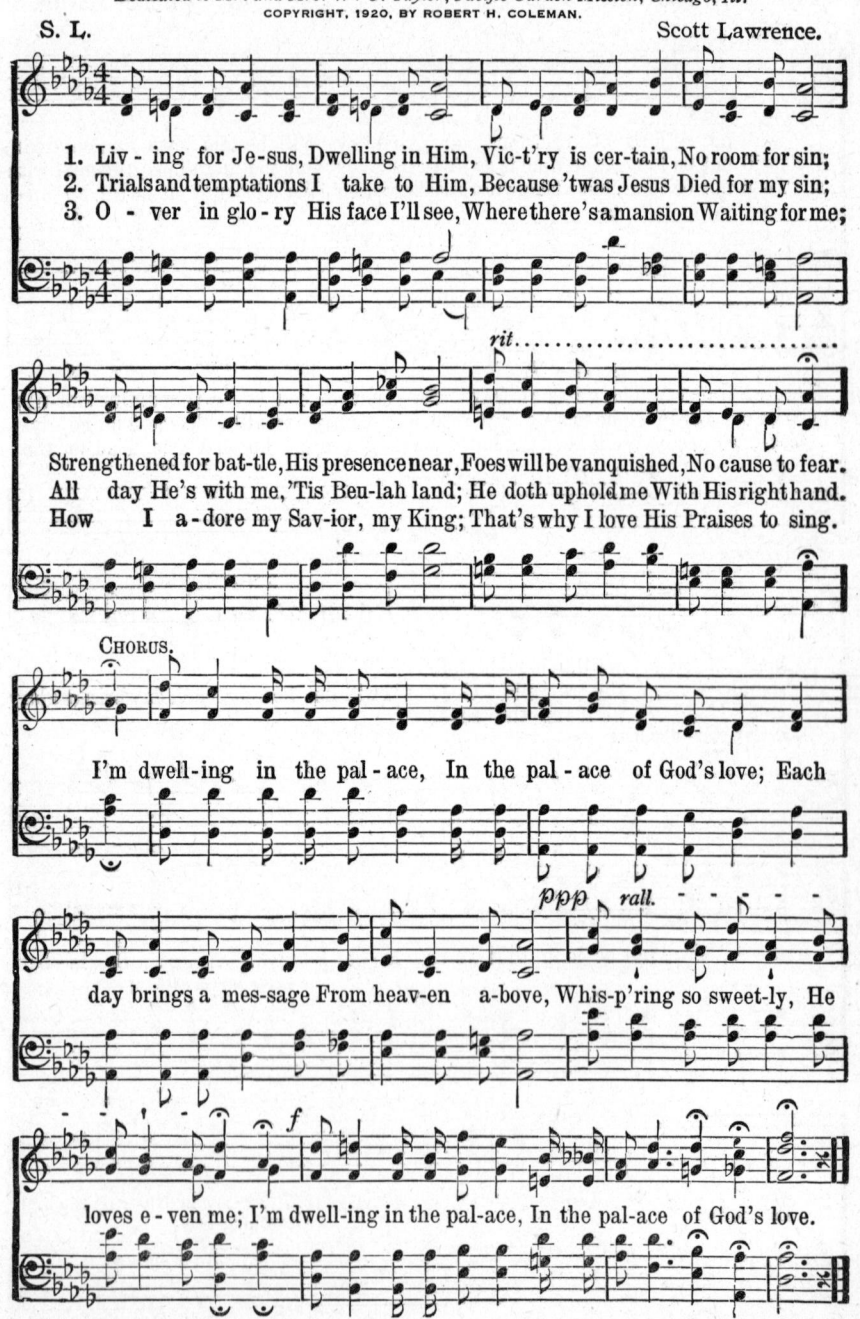

COPYRIGHT, 1920, BY ROBERT H. COLEMAN.

S. L.
Scott Lawrence.

1. Liv-ing for Je-sus, Dwelling in Him, Vic-t'ry is cer-tain, No room for sin;
2. Trials and temptations I take to Him, Because 'twas Jesus Died for my sin;
3. O - ver in glo - ry His face I'll see, Where there's a mansion Waiting for me;

Strengthened for bat-tle, His presence near, Foes will be vanquished, No cause to fear.
All day He's with me, 'Tis Beu-lah land; He doth uphold me With His right hand.
How I a-dore my Sav-ior, my King; That's why I love His Praises to sing.

CHORUS.

I'm dwell-ing in the pal-ace, In the pal-ace of God's love; Each day brings a mes-sage From heav-en a-bove, Whis-p'ring so sweet-ly, He loves e-ven me; I'm dwell-ing in the pal-ace, In the pal-ace of God's love.

164 He Loves Even Me.

S. L.
COPYRIGHT, 1914, BY E. O. EXCELL.
WORDS AND MUSIC.
Scott Lawrence.

1. When I think of my Sav-ior's great love, In com-ing from Heav-en a-bove, To die on the tree For a sin-ner like me, I am sure that He loves e-ven me.
2. When I think of the thorns on His brow, Seems as if I can see Je-sus now, As He suffered for me, That my soul might be free: I am sure that He loves e-ven me.
3. When I think how He saves me from sin, Though oft-en un-grate-ful I've been, My vow I re-new, "To be faith-ful and true:" I am sure that He loves e-ven me.

Chorus.

I am sure that He loves e-ven me, . . . I am sure that He loves e-ven me; . . . And His love is so sweet, Makes my joy so com-plete When I think how He loves e-ven me. . . . A-MEN.

165. Out of the Deep.

J. P. S.
Bass Solo.
COPYRIGHT, 1916, BY ROBERT H. COLEMAN.
J. P. Scholfield.

1. I call un-to Thee, O Lord, out of the deep; Oh, hear Thou my fee-ble prayer and guard and keep, For life with fierce temp-ta-tions does a-bound And Sa-tan casts his snares a-round; Thou, who dost nev-er sleep, Hear my call from out the deep!

2. I cry un-to Thee, O Lord, out of the deep; Wilt Thou, then each day and hour Thy vig-il keep? For I am ev-er prone to go a-stray, And with-out Thee I'd lose my way; Thou, who dost nev-er sleep, Hear my cry from out the deep!

3. I look un-to Thee, O Lord, out of the deep; Oh, make me like Him who did o'er sin-ners weep; Oh, let me take some lost one by the hand And point him to a bet-ter land; Thou, who dost nev-er sleep, Hear my prayer from out the deep!

166 Speak To My Heart.

Gene Routh.
COPYRIGHT, 1927, BY ROBERT H. COLEMAN.
INTERNATIONAL COPYRIGHT SECURED.
B. B. McKinney.

1. Speak to my heart, Lord Jesus, Speak that my soul may hear;
Speak to my heart, Lord Jesus, Calm ev-'ry doubt and fear.
2. Speak to my heart, Lord Jesus, Purge me from ev-'ry sin;
Speak to my heart, Lord Jesus, Help me the lost to win.
3. Speak to my heart, Lord Jesus, It is no longer mine;
Speak to my heart, Lord Jesus, I would be wholly Thine.

CHORUS.

Speak to my heart, oh, speak to my heart, Speak to my heart, I pray;
Yielded and still, seeking Thy will, Oh, speak to my heart to-day.

167 Where We'll Never Grow Old.

Rev. W. W. Baily.
COPYRIGHT, 1885, BY I. N. McHOSE.
I. N. McHose.

1. O have you not heard of that coun-try a-bove, The name of its King and His in-fi-nite love? His chil-dren are deathless and hap-py I'm told;
2. A man-sion of won-der-ful beau-ty is there, And Je-sus that man-sion has gone to pre-pare; Its bright jas-per walls how I long to be-hold,
3. They tell me its friend-ships and love are so pure, Its joys nev-er die, and its treasures are sure; And loved ones de-part-ed, so si-lent and cold,
4. In life's wea-ry con-flicts, there's fainting and care, Each year the gray deep-ens a shade in the hair; But in the blest book where my name is enrolled,

D. S.—*It glad-dens my heart with a joy that's un-told,*

FINE. CHORUS

Oh, will it a-bide—will we nev-er grow old?
And join in the song that will nev-er grow old. 'Twill al-ways be new, it will
Will greet us a-gain where we'll nev-er grow old.
I read of that land where we'll nev-er grow old.

To think of that land where we'll never grow old.

D. S.

nev-er de-cay; No night ev-er comes, it will al-ways be day;

168 Deep Down In My Heart.

Rev. W. C. Poole.   COPYRIGHT, 1930, BY ROBERT H. COLEMAN.   B. D. Ackley.
INTERNATIONAL COPYRIGHT SECURED.

Solo

1. Deep down in my heart there is gladness to-day, Way down, deep in my heart;
2. Deep down in my heart there is wonderful peace, Way down, deep in my heart,
3. Deep down in my heart there are blessings untold, Way down, deep in my heart,
4. Deep down in my heart there is heaven with-in, Way down, deep in my heart,

Accomp.

For Je-sus has come in, for-ev-er to stay, Way down, deep in my heart.
That thro' all the a-ges will ev-er in-crease, Way down, deep in my heart.
More pre-cious than silver, or diamonds or gold, Way down, deep in my heart.
Where Je-sus is liv-ing, and drives away sin, Way down, deep in my heart.

Refrain

Way down, deep in my heart, Way down, deep in my heart; Filling my soul with His love ev-'ry day, Way down, way down, deep in my heart.

SM-6

169. Because of You.

B. B. McK.
B. B. McKinney.

COPYRIGHT, 1932, BY ROBERT H. COLEMAN.
INTERNATIONAL COPYRIGHT SECURED.

1. In a land of sin and doubt, Where the Master's crowd-ed out, Do you stand a-mong the faith-ful, brave and true? Do you live for God and right, Do you fal-ter in the fight, Is the world a bet-ter place because of you?
2. Lonely hearts are sad and drear, Long-ing for a word of cheer, They have lost the joy in Je-sus they once knew; Do you light-ly pass them by, Are you heedless of their cry, Is the world a bet-ter place because of you?
3. Man-y lost ones in the night Turn their eyes to-ward your light; Does its gleam re-flect the Sav-ior kind and true? Does it lead them to His side, Do you in His will a-bide, Is the world a bet-ter place because of you?

CHORUS.

Is the world a bet-ter place be-cause of you? . . . Do you stand among the faithful, brave and true? . . . Can the lost see Christ in you, the brave and true? be-cause of you?

Because of You.

Does your life ring true, Is the world a better place because of you?... of you?

---

170 ## Nothing Between.

COPYRIGHT, 1905, BY C. A. TINDLEY.

Words and Music by C. A. Tindley.   Arr. by F. A. Clark.

1. Nothing between my soul and the Savior, Naught of this world's delusive dream; I have renounced all sinful pleasure, Jesus is mine; let nothing between.
2. Nothing between like worldly pleasure; Habits of life, though harmless they seem, Must not my heart from Him ever sever,— He is my all, let nothing between.
3. Nothing between, e'en many hard trials, Though the whole world against me convene; Watching with prayer and much self-denial, I'll triumph at last, with nothing between.

Fine **Chorus.**

Nothing between my soul and the Savior, So that His blessed face may be seen; Nothing preventing the least of His favor,

D. S.—Keep the way clear! Let nothing between.

171. God Leads Us Along.

G. A. Y.

Copyright, 1931, by G. A. Young, Renewal.
Lillenas Publishing Co., Owner. Used by Permission.

G. A. Young.

1. In shad-y, green pas-tures, so rich and so sweet, God leads His dear chil-dren a-long; Where the wa-ter's cold flow bathes the wea-ry one's feet,
2. Sometimes on the mount where the sun shines so bright, God leads His dear chil-dren a-long; Some-times in the val-ley in the dark-est of night,
3. Tho' sor-rows be-fall us, and Sa-tan op-pose, God leads His dear chil-dren a-long; Through grace we can con-quer, de-feat all our foes,
4. A-way from the mire, and a-way from the clay, God leads His dear chil-dren a-long; A - - way up in glo-ry, e-ter-ni-ty's day,

Chorus

God leads His dear chil-dren a-long. Some thro' the waters, some thro' the flood, Some thro' the fire, but all thro' the Blood; Some thro' great sor-row, but God gives a song, In the night sea-son and all the day long.

172. Back to Bethel.

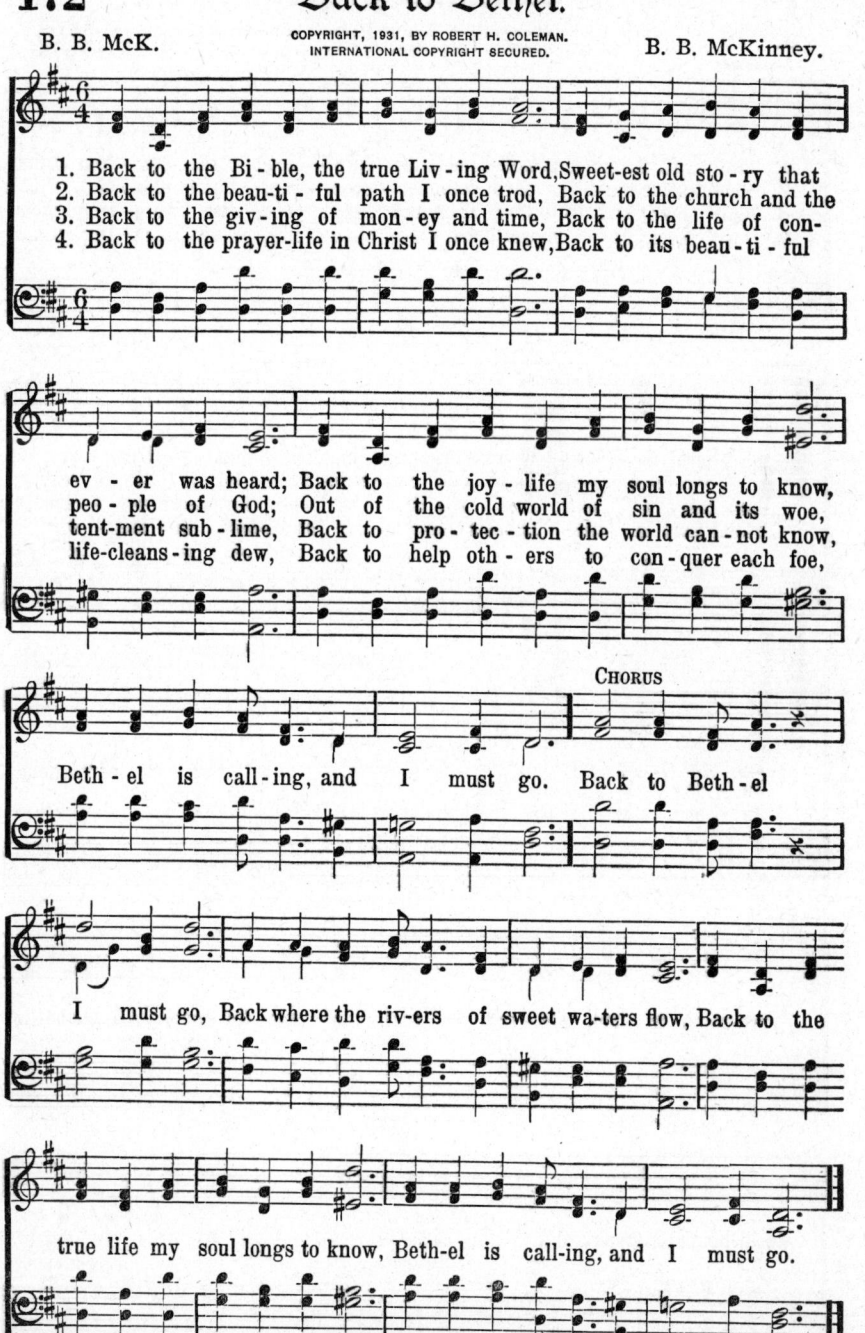

B. B. McK.
COPYRIGHT, 1931, BY ROBERT H. COLEMAN.
INTERNATIONAL COPYRIGHT SECURED.
B. B. McKinney.

1. Back to the Bi-ble, the true Liv-ing Word, Sweet-est old sto-ry that ev-er was heard; Back to the joy-life my soul longs to know,
2. Back to the beau-ti-ful path I once trod, Back to the church and the peo-ple of God; Out of the cold world of sin and its woe,
3. Back to the giv-ing of mon-ey and time, Back to the life of con-tent-ment sub-lime, Back to pro-tec-tion the world can-not know,
4. Back to the prayer-life in Christ I once knew, Back to its beau-ti-ful life-cleans-ing dew, Back to help oth-ers to con-quer each foe,

CHORUS

Beth-el is call-ing, and I must go. Back to Beth-el I must go, Back where the riv-ers of sweet wa-ters flow, Back to the true life my soul longs to know, Beth-el is call-ing, and I must go.

173 Jesus is Real and Precious to Me.

H. G. T.
INTERNATIONAL COPYRIGHT, 1922, BY HERBERT G. TOVEY
ROBERT H. COLEMAN, OWNER.
Herbert G. Tovey.

SOLO.

1. Tho' all things this world holds as pre-cious Are ta-ken from me here be-low, There's one pre-cious truth that I treas-ure,
2. Should some earth-ly care come op-press-ing, Some cloud thro' which I can-not see, I've one con-stant Friend, it is Je-sus,
3. A-lone, and a-way from my loved ones, No words from their lips can I hear; And yet there is One far more pre-cious,
4. O soul, in this world ev-er chang-ing, Now seek-ing some friend that is true, There's One who is stead-fast, un-fail-ing,

CHORUS.

Je-sus is real, this I know.
He is as real as can be.
Je-sus is real, and is near.
Je-sus is real; He seeks you.

Je-sus is real and pre-cious to me, Je-sus is real to me; (to me;) All that the world holds as treas-ure may go, But Je-sus is real to me. (to me.)

174 Satisfied With Jesus.

B. B. McK.
B. B. McKinney.

COPYRIGHT, 1926, BY ROBERT H. COLEMAN.
INTERNATIONAL COPYRIGHT SECURED.

Slowly.

1. I am sat-is-fied with Je-sus, He has done so much for me,
2. He is with me in my tri-als, Best of friends of all is He;
3. I can hear the voice of Je-sus Call-ing out so plead-ing-ly,
4. When my work on earth is end-ed, And I cross the mys-tic sea,

He has suf-fered to re-deem me, He has died to set me free.
I can al-ways count on Je-sus, Can He al-ways count on me?
"Go and win the lost and stray-ing;" Is He sat-is-fied with me?
Oh, that I could hear Him say-ing, "I am sat-is-fied with thee."

CHORUS.

I am sat-is-fied, I am sat-is-fied, I am sat-is-fied with Je-sus, But the ques-tion comes to me, As I think of Cal-va-ry, Is my Mas-ter sat-is-fied with me?

175 Some Day, It Won't Be Long.

COPYRIGHT, 1910, BY CHARLIE D. TILLMAN.

L. B. B.
L. B. Bridgers.

1. Some day I'll cross the mys-tic stream, It won't be long, it may be soon;
2. Some day this mor-tal life shall cease, It won't be long, it may be soon;
3. He's com-ing back with glo-ry rare, It won't be long, it may be soon;
4. Then as you trav-el on life's way, Thro' waters deep, or bil-lows' foam;

Some day I'll lay my bur-dens down, It won't be long, it may be soon;
Some day I'll see my Sav-ior's face, It won't be long, it may be soon;
We'll rise to meet Him in the air, It won't be long, it may be soon;
You may have Je-sus as your stay, He'll walk with you and lead you home.

Some day I'll reach the gold-en shore, And dwell with Je-sus ev-er-more,
Some day I'll leave this vale of tears, For-get the strug-gles of long years,
If He should call me, this I know: I'm saved and read-y now to go,
O broth-er, will you let Him in? He'll save and keep you free from sin,

I'll meet the ones who've gone be-fore, It won't be long, it may be soon.
I'll know no sor-row, pain, nor fears; It won't be long, it may be soon.
I'm wait-ing with my heart a-glow; It won't be long, it may be soon.
Till heav-en's door you en-ter in; It won't be long, it may be soon.

※ Sing after last verse. FINE.   D. S.

D.S.—There'll be no sorrow there. There'll be no sorrow there, In heav'n above, where all is love,

176 He'll Never Forget to Keep Me.

COPYRIGHT, 1899, BY F. A. GRAVES.   USED BY PERMISSION.

F. A. Graves.   F. A. Graves.

DUET. *Tenor and Alto.*

1. My Father has man-y dear chil-dren; Will He ev-er for-get to keep me?
2. Our Father remembers the spar-rows, Their val-ue and fall He doth see;
3. The words of the Lord are so price-less, How pa-tient and watchful is He;
4. O broth-er, why don't you ac-cept Him? He of-fers sal-va-tion so free;

He gave His own Son to re-deem them, And He can-not for-get to keep me.
But dear-er to Him are His chil-dren, And He'll nev-er for-get to keep me.
Tho' moth-er for-get her own off-spring, Yet He'll nev-er for-get to keep me.
Re-pent and be-lieve and o-bey Him, And He'll nev-er for-get to keep thee.

REFRAIN.

1-3. He'll nev-er for-get to keep me (keep me), He'll nev-er for-get to keep me (keep me);
4. He'll nev-er for-get to keep thee (keep thee), He'll nev-er for-get to keep thee (keep thee);

He gave His own Son to re-deem me, And He'll nev-er for-get to keep me.
But dear-er to Him are His chil-dren, And He'll nev-er for-get to keep me.
Tho' moth-er for-get her own off-spring, Yet He'll nev-er for-get to keep me.
Re-pent and be-lieve and o-bey Him, And He'll nev-er for-get to keep thee.

177 Wonderful Love.

COPYRIGHT, 1922, BY ROBERT H. COLEMAN AND ROBERT HARKNESS.
INTERNATIONAL COPYRIGHT SECURED.

R. H.
Robert Harkness.

SOLO OR UNISON. *Moderato.*

1. How wondrous the love of my Sav-ior to me, In giv-ing His life up-on Cal-va-ry's tree;
2. How great was the sac-ri-fice made once for all, When Christ on the cross answered God's divine call;
3. How ful-ly complete is the work of the cross, It cleans-es the heart of its sin-stain and dross;

rit.

I nev-er could mer-it this gift of God's grace, That made Him my Savior, my sin to ef-face.
I mar-vel to think that for me Je-sus died,'Twas love gave my Savior to be cru-ci-fied.
Sal-va-tion is of-fered to those who be-lieve, To all who trust Jesus and God's Word receive.

CHORUS. *a tempo.*

Oh, won-der-ful love of my Sav - ior, Such won-der-ful love to be-stow;......
Won - der - ful love of my Sav - ior, my Sav-ior to me;
Won - der - ful love of my Sav-ior to me, of my Sav-ior to me;
Won - der - ful love of my Sav - ior, my Sav-ior to me;

Why He should die on Cal-va-ry, Why give His life to set me free, I

Wonderful Love.

cres. — *rit.* *ad lib.* *ff*

can-not tell, I do not know! But it is so! Yes, it is so!

178 The Wayfaring Pilgrim.

Words arr.
ARRANGEMENT COPYRIGHT, 1925, BY B. B. McKINNEY.
ROBERT H. COLEMAN, OWNER.
Arr. B. B. McKinney.

1. I am a poor way-far-ing pil-grim, While trav'ling thro' this world below;
2. I know dark clouds will gather o'er me, I know my pathway's rough and steep;
3. I'll soon be free from ev-'ry tri-al, This form will rest be-neath the sod;

There is no sick-ness, toil, nor dan-ger In that bright world to which I go.
But gold-en fields lie out be-fore me, Where weary eyes no more shall weep.
I'll drop the cross of self-de-ni-al, And en-ter in my home with God.

I'm go-ing there to meet my fa-ther, I'm go-ing there no more to roam;
I'm go-ing there to see my moth-er, She said she'd meet me when I come;
I'm go-ing there to see my Sav-ior, Who shed for me His pre-cious blood;

CHORUS.

I am just go-ing o-ver Jor-dan, I am just go-ing o-ver home.

179 I Can See the Lights of Home.

Miss Calia Altstaetter. COPYRIGHT, 1926, BY ROBERT H. COLEMAN. INTERNATIONAL COPYRIGHT SECURED. B. B. McKinney.

1. There's a home of man-y man-sions in the Fa-ther's house a-bove,
2. When the storms of life are rag-ing, doubts and fears my soul as-sail,
3. When the shades of night are fall-ing, and my loved ones have passed on,

That our Sav-ior is pre-par-ing for the chil-dren of His love;
His "Let not your heart be troub-led," I can hear a-bove the gale;
And I'm wait-ing glad, ex-pect-ant, wait-ing for the heav'n-ly dawn,

So my heart knows not de-spair-ing, tho' in sor-row oft I roam,
So with face turned ev-er home-ward, while the bil-lows dash and foam,
Brighter, bright-er, ev-er bright-er, till the an-gels for me come,

Gleam-ing from the man-y man-sions, I can see the lights of home.
Gleam-ing from the man-y man-sions, I can see the lights of home.
Gleam-ing from the man-y man-sions, I can see the lights of home.

CHORUS.

I can see the lights of home, I can see the lights of home, Gleaming from the many

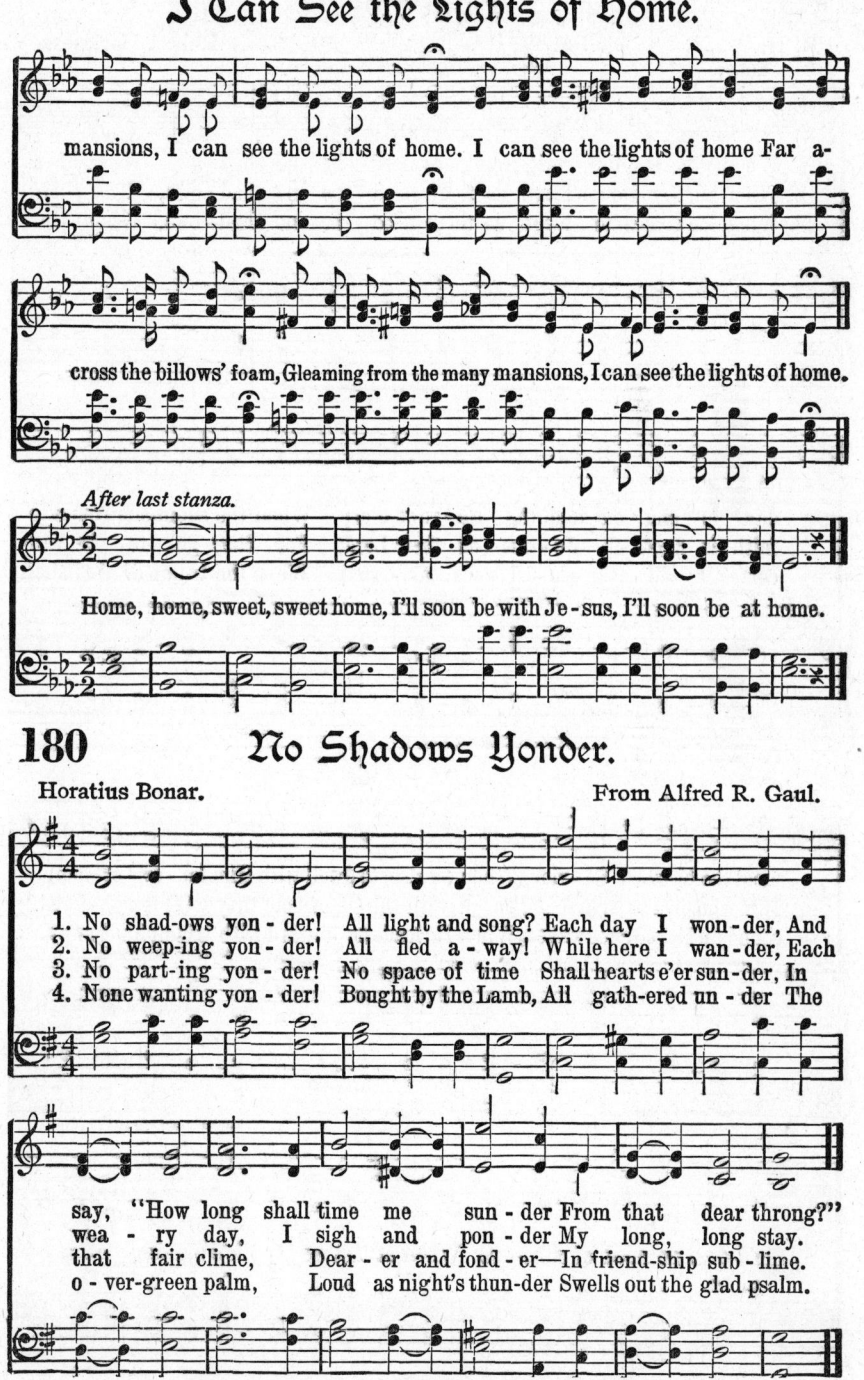

I Can See the Lights of Home.

mansions, I can see the lights of home. I can see the lights of home Far across the billows' foam, Gleaming from the many mansions, I can see the lights of home.

After last stanza.

Home, home, sweet, sweet home, I'll soon be with Je-sus, I'll soon be at home.

180 No Shadows Yonder.

Horatius Bonar.   From Alfred R. Gaul.

1. No shad-ows yon-der! All light and song? Each day I won-der, And say, "How long shall time me sun-der From that dear throng?"
2. No weep-ing yon-der! All fled a-way! While here I wan-der, Each wea-ry day, I sigh and pon-der My long, long stay.
3. No part-ing yon-der! No space of time Shall hearts e'er sun-der, In that fair clime, Dear-er and fond-er—In friend-ship sub-lime.
4. None wanting yon-der! Bought by the Lamb, All gath-ered un-der The o-ver-green palm, Loud as night's thun-der Swells out the glad psalm.

181 Shadows.

Robert Harkness.

1. When we cross the val-ley there need be no shad-ows, When life's
day is end-ed and its sor-rows o'er; When the summons comes to
meet the bless-ed Sa-vior, When we rise to dwell with Him for-ev-er-more.

2. When our loved ones leave us there need be no shad-ows, If their
faith is fixed in Je-sus as their Lord; For they go to be with
Him who died to save them, To be with the One whom they have long a-dored.

3. When He comes to meet us there need be no shad-ows, When He
comes in all His glo-ri-ous ar-ray; When the trump of God shall
sound and loved ones waken, When He leads us onward with triumphant sway.

CHORUS.

Shad-ows! no need of shad-ows When at last we lay life's bur-den down;

Shadows.

Shad-ows! no need of shad-ows When at last we gain the vic-tor's crown!

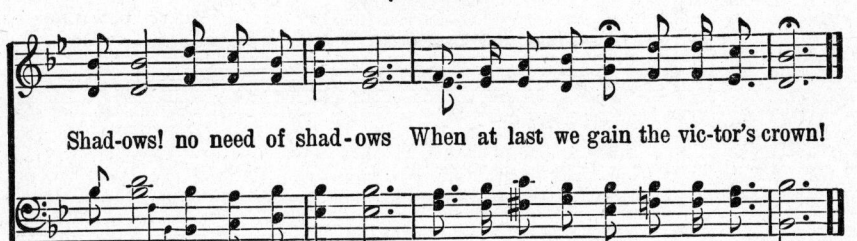

182 Sometime!

R. H.
DUET.

COPYRIGHT, 1922, BY ROB'T H. COLEMAN & ROBERT HARKNESS.
INTERNATIONAL COPYRIGHT SECURED.
OWNED BY ROBERT H. COLEMAN

Robert Harkness.

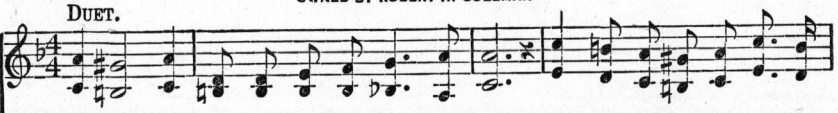

1. Some-time all sor-rows shall be o'er, Some-time! All earth-ly care be known no
2. Some-time our loved ones we shall greet, Some-time! When in the Father's house we
3. Some-time when sets at last life's sun, Some-time! Our jour-ney end-ed, la-bor
4. Some-time, I know not when 'twill be, Some-time! My Lord will come a-gain for

more! Oh, what re-joic-ing on the golden shore,
meet, On - ly to sit for - ev - er at His feet, Some-time, some-time soon!
done, Oh, what a crown for ev-'ry vic-t'ry won, some-time soon!
me, Then I shall reign with Him e-ter-nal-ly,

183. No Disappointment in Heaven.

F. M. L.
COPYRIGHT, 1914, BY F. M. LEHMAN.
HOMER A. RODEHEAVER, OWNER.
F. M. Lehman.
Har. by Miss Claudia Lehman.

1. There's no dis-ap-point-ment in heav-en, No wea-ri-ness, sor-row or pain; No hearts that are bleed-ing and bro-ken, No song with a mi-nor re-frain; The clouds of our earth-ly ho-ri-zon Will nev-er ap-pear in the sky, For all will be sun-shine and glad-ness, With nev-er a sob nor a sigh.

2. We'll nev-er pay rent for our man-sion, The tax-es will nev-er come due; Our gar-ments will nev-er grow thread-bare, But al-ways be fade-less and new; We'll nev-er be hun-gry nor thirst-y, Nor lan-guish in pov-er-ty there, For all the rich boun-ties of heav-en His sanc-ti-fied chil-dren will share.

3. There'll nev-er be crepe on the door-knob, No fu-ner-al train in the sky; No graves on the hill-sides of glo-ry, For there we shall nev-er-more die; The old will be young there for-ev-er, Trans-formed in a mo-ment of time; Im-mor-tal we'll stand in His like-ness, The stars and the sun to out-shine.

No Disappointment in Heaven.

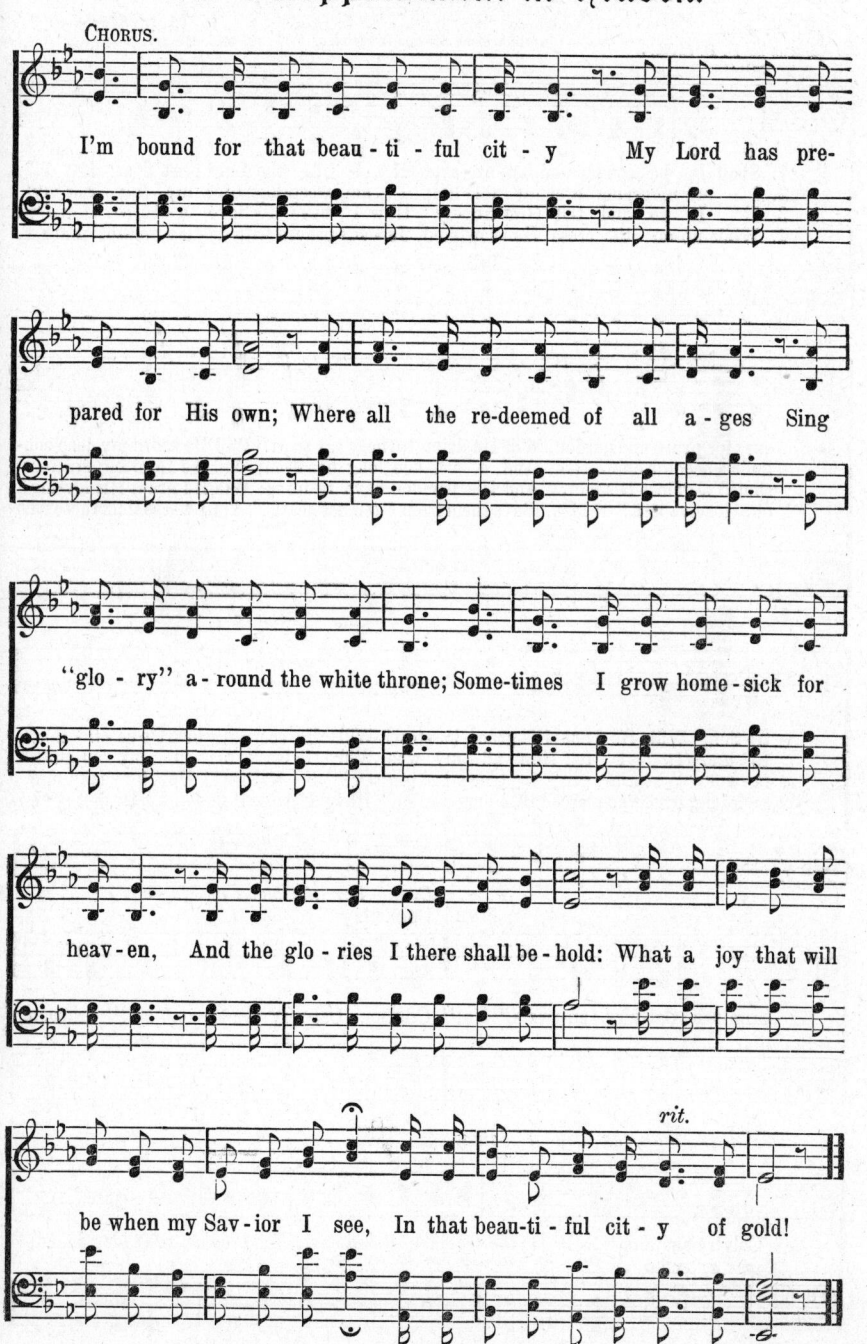

Chorus.

I'm bound for that beau-ti-ful cit-y My Lord has pre-pared for His own; Where all the re-deemed of all a-ges Sing "glo-ry" a-round the white throne; Some-times I grow home-sick for heav-en, And the glo-ries I there shall be-hold: What a joy that will be when my Sav-ior I see, In that beau-ti-ful cit-y of gold!

184 Crimson Calvary Answers, "No!"

W. T. Dale.
Chorus by B. B. McK.

COPYRIGHT, 1932, BY ROBERT H. COLEMAN.
INTERNATIONAL COPYRIGHT SECURED.

B. B. McKinney.

Solo.

1. Shall I be condemned for-ev-er, If I to the Lord draw near; If I
2. I am mourning o'er my fol-lies; I am weep-ing o'er my sin; For my
3. If I go and tell Him tru-ly How I have His love a-bused, How I've
4. While up-on the cross He suf-fered, Je-sus prayed with dy-ing breath, "Father,

sue for peace and pardon, Will He deign to hear my prayer? Will He scorn my deep con-
guilt's become oppressive, And a bur-den long has been; Will the Lord be gracious
sinned a-gainst His mercy, And His par-don have re-fused; Will He grant His lov-ing
oh, forgive them," cried He, "Save them from e-ter-nal death;" Am I worse than those who

tri-tion, Will He not His grace be-stow? Will He scorn my heart's pe-ti-tion?
to me, If I tell Him all my woe, Will He leave me in my an-guish?
fa-vor When in pen-i-tence I go; Or in wrath will He for-sake me?
mocked Him, And who pierced Him long a-go, Have I passed be-yond His mer-cy?

D. S.—*For the blood of Je-sus cleans-es*

Fine. Chorus.

Crim-son Cal-v'ry an-swers, "No!" Crimson Cal-v'ry an-swers, "No!" Crimson

Whit-er than the driv-en snow.

Calv'ry answers, "No!" On the cross the blessed Savior Paid the sin-price long a-go;

Crimson Calvary Answers, "No!"

D.S. All who will on Him believe, Full redemption shall receive,

185 Return.

B. B. McK.
COPYRIGHT, 1932, BY ROBERT H. COLEMAN.
INTERNATIONAL COPYRIGHT SECURED.
B. B. McKinney.

Solo.

1. O soul, far away from the beau-ti-ful fold, Re-turn, re-turn, re-turn!
2. There's shelter and food in the pal-ace of God, Re-turn, re-turn, re-turn!
3. Tho' sin-sick, un-wor-thy to en-ter the door, Re-turn, re-turn, re-turn!

Why lon-ger re-main in the storm and the cold? Re-turn, re-turn, re-turn!
True joy you will find in the path you once trod, Re-turn, re-turn, re-turn!
Your sins He'll forgive and re-mem-ber no more, Re-turn, re-turn, re-turn!

CHORUS.

Return un-to Christ, He'll return un-to you, A wel-come a-waits you, so tender and true; The joy of salvation in you He'll renew, Re-turn, re-turn, re-turn!

186 My Father Watches Over Me.

Rev. W. C. Martin.
COPYRIGHT, 1910, BY CHAS. H. GABRIEL.
HOMER A. RODEHEAVER, OWNER.
Chas. H. Gabriel.

1. I trust in God wher-ev-er I may be,...... Up-on the land or on the roll-ing sea, For, come what may, From day to day, My heav'nly
2. He makes the rose an ob-ject of His care,.... He guides the ea-gle thro' the pathless air, And sure-ly He Re-mem-bers me,—My heav'nly
3. I trust in God, for, in the li-on's den,...... On bat-tle-field, or in the pris-on pen, Thro' praise or blame, Thro' flood or flame, My heav'nly
4. The val-ley may be dark, the shad-ows deep,.... But O, the Shep-herd guards His lonely sheep; And thro' the gloom He'll lead me home, My heav'nly

Fa-ther watch-es o - ver me.

CHORUS.

I trust in God,—I know He cares for me,............ On moun-tain bleak or on the storm-y
He cares for me, On moun-tain bleak or on the

sea;............ Tho' bil-lows roll,............... He keeps my
sea, the storm-y sea; Tho' bil-lows roll, He

My Father Watches Over Me.

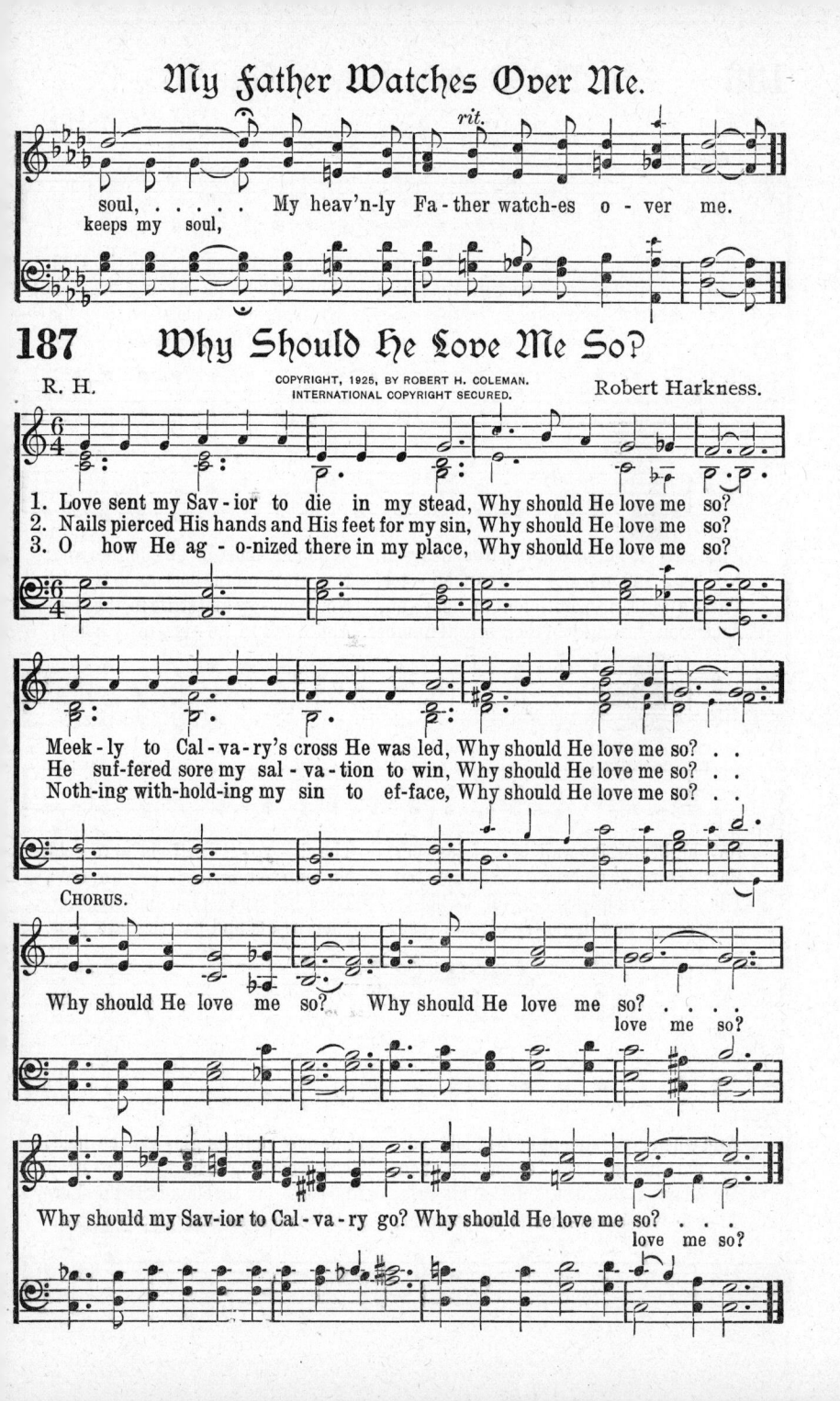

rit.

soul, ... My heav'n-ly Fa-ther watch-es o - ver me.
keeps my soul,

187 Why Should He Love Me So?

R. H.   COPYRIGHT, 1925, BY ROBERT H. COLEMAN.   Robert Harkness.
INTERNATIONAL COPYRIGHT SECURED.

1. Love sent my Sav-ior to die in my stead, Why should He love me so?
2. Nails pierced His hands and His feet for my sin, Why should He love me so?
3. O how He ag-o-nized there in my place, Why should He love me so?

Meek-ly to Cal-va-ry's cross He was led, Why should He love me so? ..
He suf-fered sore my sal - va-tion to win, Why should He love me so? ..
Noth-ing with-hold-ing my sin to ef-face, Why should He love me so? ..

CHORUS.

Why should He love me so? Why should He love me so? ....
love me so?

Why should my Sav-ior to Cal-va-ry go? Why should He love me so? ...
love me so?

188. The Pearly White City.

A. F. I.
Copyright, 1929, by Arthur F. Ingler, Renewal.
Lillenas Publishing Co., Owner. Used by Permission.
Arthur F. Ingler.

Moderato.

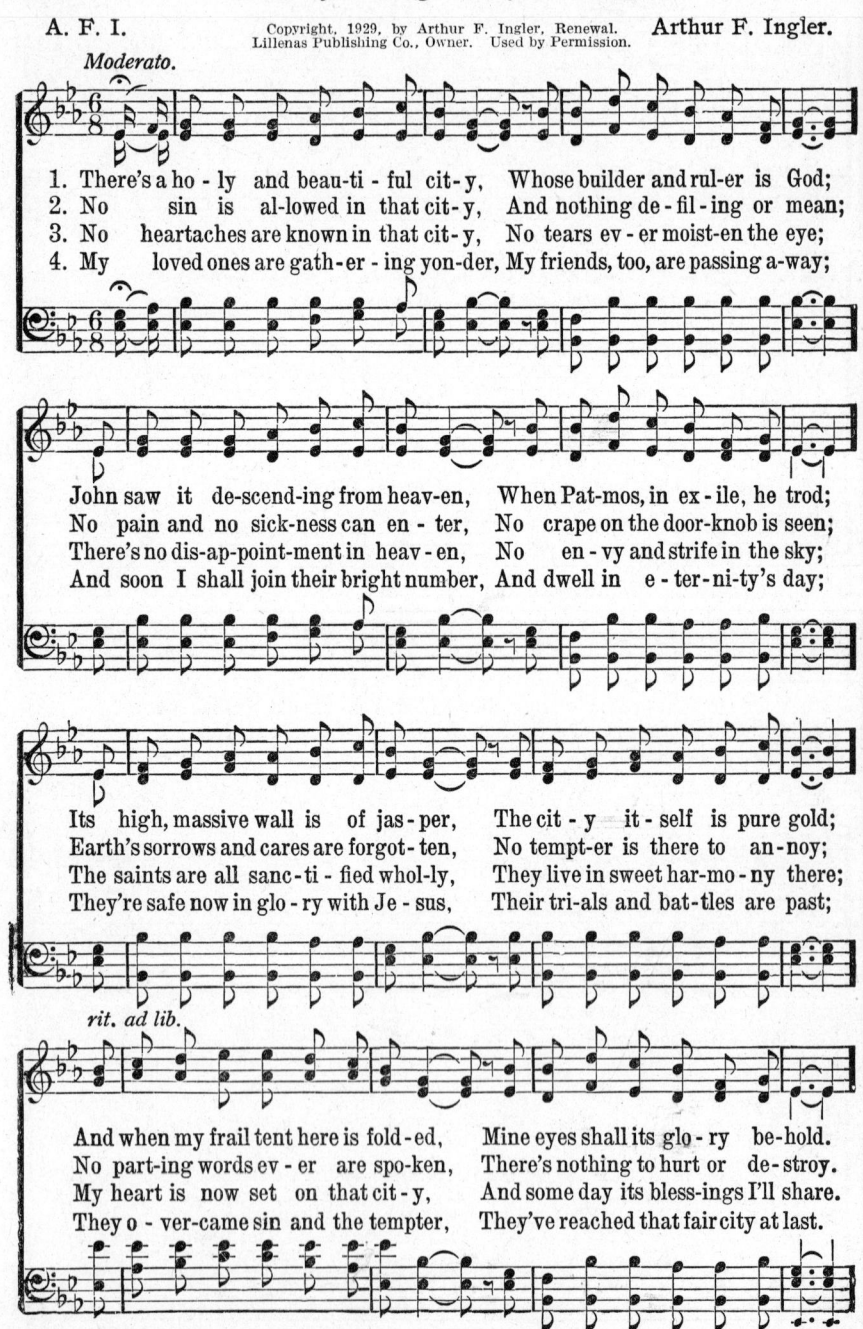

1. There's a ho-ly and beau-ti-ful cit-y, Whose builder and rul-er is God;
2. No sin is al-lowed in that cit-y, And nothing de-fil-ing or mean;
3. No heartaches are known in that cit-y, No tears ev-er moist-en the eye;
4. My loved ones are gath-er-ing yon-der, My friends, too, are passing a-way;

John saw it de-scend-ing from heav-en, When Pat-mos, in ex-ile, he trod;
No pain and no sick-ness can en-ter, No crape on the door-knob is seen;
There's no dis-ap-point-ment in heav-en, No en-vy and strife in the sky;
And soon I shall join their bright number, And dwell in e-ter-ni-ty's day;

Its high, massive wall is of jas-per, The cit-y it-self is pure gold;
Earth's sorrows and cares are forgot-ten, No tempt-er is there to an-noy;
The saints are all sanc-ti-fied whol-ly, They live in sweet har-mo-ny there;
They're safe now in glo-ry with Je-sus, Their tri-als and bat-tles are past;

rit. ad lib.

And when my frail tent here is fold-ed, Mine eyes shall its glo-ry be-hold.
No part-ing words ev-er are spo-ken, There's nothing to hurt or de-stroy.
My heart is now set on that cit-y, And some day its bless-ings I'll share.
They o-ver-came sin and the tempter, They've reached that fair city at last.

The Pearly White City.

REFRAIN. *Slow.*

In that bright cit-y,.. pearl-y white cit-y,.. I have a man-sion, an harp, and a crown; Now I am watch-ing, wait-ing, and long-ing, For the white cit-y that's soon com-ing down. A-MEN.

rit.

189 Softly Now the Light of Day.

Geo. W. Doane.   *Seymour. 7s.*   Carl M. von Weber.

1. Soft - ly now the light of day Fades up - on our sight a - way;
2. Thou whose all - per - vad - ing eye Naught es - capes, with-out, with - in,
3. Soon for us the light of day Shall for - ev - er pass a - way;

Free from care, from la - bor free, Lord, we would com-mune with Thee!
Par - don each in - firm - i - ty, O - pen fault and se - cret sin!
Then, from sin and sor - row free, Take us, Lord, to dwell with Thee!

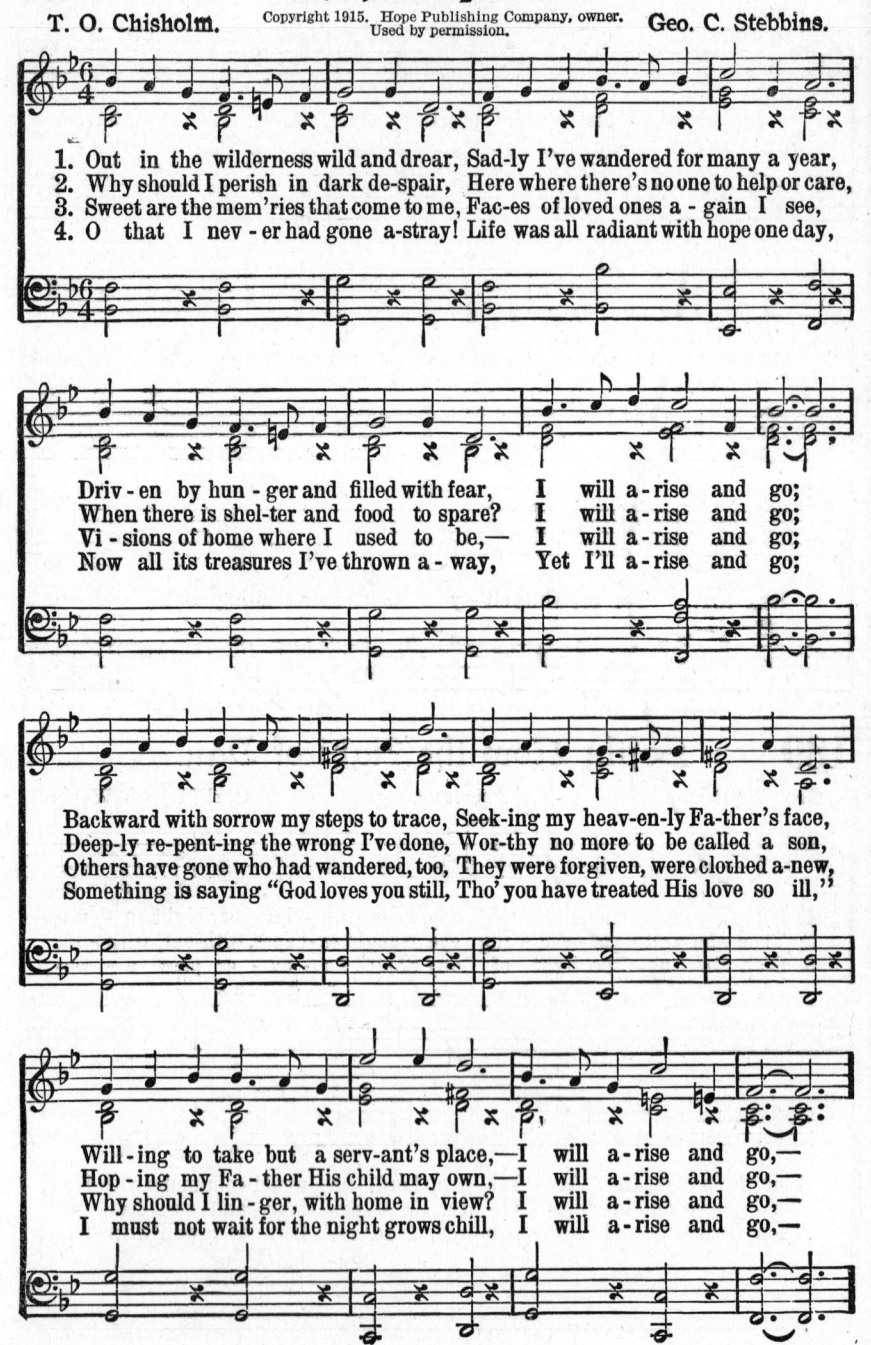

190 The Prodigal Son.

T. O. Chisholm.
Geo. C. Stebbins.
Copyright 1915. Hope Publishing Company, owner. Used by permission.

1. Out in the wilderness wild and drear, Sad-ly I've wandered for many a year,
2. Why should I perish in dark de-spair, Here where there's no one to help or care,
3. Sweet are the mem'ries that come to me, Fac-es of loved ones a-gain I see,
4. O that I nev-er had gone a-stray! Life was all radiant with hope one day,

Driv-en by hun-ger and filled with fear, I will a-rise and go;
When there is shel-ter and food to spare? I will a-rise and go;
Vi-sions of home where I used to be,— I will a-rise and go;
Now all its treasures I've thrown a-way, Yet I'll a-rise and go;

Backward with sorrow my steps to trace, Seek-ing my heav-en-ly Fa-ther's face,
Deep-ly re-pent-ing the wrong I've done, Wor-thy no more to be called a son,
Others have gone who had wandered, too, They were forgiven, were clothed a-new,
Something is saying "God loves you still, Tho' you have treated His love so ill,"

Will-ing to take but a serv-ant's place,—I will a-rise and go,—
Hop-ing my Fa-ther His child may own,—I will a-rise and go,—
Why should I lin-ger, with home in view? I will a-rise and go,—
I must not wait for the night grows chill, I will a-rise and go,—

The Prodigal Son.

CHORUS.

Back to my Father and home, Back to my Father and home, and home,
I will arise and go Back to my Father and home.
and go

191   I Will Arise and Go to Jesus.

J. Hart.   *Arise. 8. 7. 8. 7. 4. 7.*   Arr.

1. Come, ye sinners, poor and needy, Weak and wounded, sick and sore;
2. Come, ye thirsty, come, and welcome, God's free bounty glorify;
3. Come, ye weary, heavy-laden, Lost and ruined by the fall;
4. Let not conscience make you linger, Nor of fitness fondly dream;

CHO.—*I will arise and go to Jesus, He will embrace me in His arms;*

D. C. for Chorus.

Jesus ready stands to save you, Full of pity, love and pow'r.
True belief and true repentance, Ev'ry grace that brings you nigh.
If you tarry till you're better, You will never come at all.
All the fitness He requireth Is to feel your need of Him. A-MEN

In the arms of my dear Savior, Oh, there are ten thousand charms.

192 One Day!

Copyright, 1910. By Chas. H. Marsh, Tabernacle Publishing Co., owner.

Rev. J. Wilbur Chapman, D.D. — Chas. H. Marsh.

1. One day when heav-en was filled with His prais-es, One day when sin was as black as could be, ... Je-sus came forth to be born of a vir-gin—Dwelt amongst men, my ex-am-ple is He! ...
2. One day they led Him up Cal-va-ry's moun-tain, One day they nailed Him to die on the tree; .. Suf-fer-ing an-guish, de-spised and re-ject-ed: Bear-ing our sins, my Re-deem-er is He! ...
3. One day they left Him a-lone in the gar-den, One day He rest-ed, from suf-fer-ing free; .. An-gels came down o'er His tomb to keep vig-il; Hope of the hope-less, my Sav-ior is He! ...
4. One day the grave could con-ceal Him no lon-ger, One day the stone rolled a-way from the door; .. Then He a-rose, o-ver death He had conquered; Now is as-cend-ed, my Lord ev-er-more!
5. One day the trump-et will sound for His com-ing, One day the skies with His glo-ries will shine; Won-der-ful day, my be-lov-ed ones bring-ing; Glo-ri-ous Sav-ior, this Je-sus is mine!

CHORUS.

Liv-ing, He loved me; dy-ing, He saved me; Bur-ied, He car-ried my sins far a-way; .. Ris-ing, He jus-ti-fied

One Day!

free-ly for-ev-er: One day He's com-ing— O glo-ri-ous day!

193 Think On Thy Way.

J. P. S.

COPYRIGHT, 1917, BY E. O. EXCELL, OWNER.
USED BY PERMISSION.

J. P. Scholfield.

1. Think on thy way, O thou storm-driv-en child; Out on the o-cean so dark and so wild, Far from thy God you are drift-ing to-day,—
2. Think on thy way: with-out Pi-lot or Guide, Far from the shore with no Friend by your side, Thought-less of Him who would fain be your stay,
3. Think on thy way, God will not let you go; His might-y arm can de-stroy ev-'ry foe; Trust Him to-day, all His man-dates o-bey;

CODA. (*After last verse only.*)

Think on thy way, think on thy way. Think on thy way, think on thy way,

Is it lead-ing you to God and home? Think on thy way. A-MEN.

194. Will the Circle Be Unbroken?

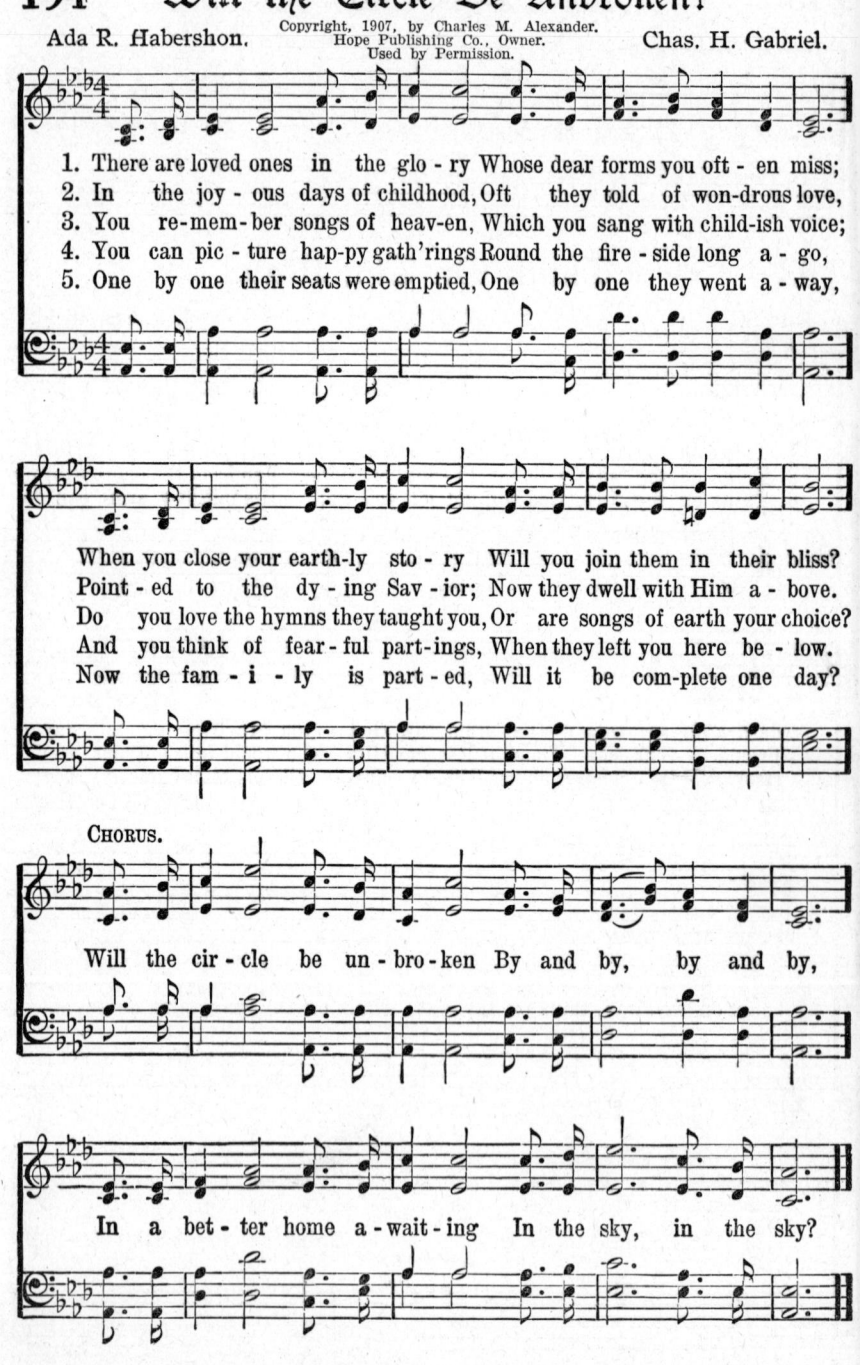

Ada R. Habershon.
Copyright, 1907, by Charles M. Alexander.
Hope Publishing Co., Owner.
Used by Permission.
Chas. H. Gabriel.

1. There are loved ones in the glo-ry Whose dear forms you oft-en miss;
2. In the joy-ous days of childhood, Oft they told of won-drous love,
3. You re-mem-ber songs of heav-en, Which you sang with child-ish voice;
4. You can pic-ture hap-py gath'rings Round the fire-side long a-go,
5. One by one their seats were emptied, One by one they went a-way,

When you close your earth-ly sto-ry Will you join them in their bliss?
Point-ed to the dy-ing Sav-ior; Now they dwell with Him a-bove.
Do you love the hymns they taught you, Or are songs of earth your choice?
And you think of fear-ful part-ings, When they left you here be-low.
Now the fam-i-ly is part-ed, Will it be com-plete one day?

CHORUS.

Will the cir-cle be un-bro-ken By and by, by and by,

In a bet-ter home a-wait-ing In the sky, in the sky?

195. The Ninety and Nine.

Elizabeth C. Clephane. COPYRIGHT, 1904, BY IRA D. SANKEY. RENEWAL. BIGLOW AND MAIN CO., OWNER. Ira D. Sankey.

1. There were ninety and nine that safe-ly lay In the shel-ter of the fold,
2. "Lord, Thou hast here Thy ninety and nine; Are they not enough for Thee?"
3. But none of the ransomed ev-er knew How deep were the waters crossed;
4. "Lord, whence are those blood-drops all the way That mark out the mountain's track?"
5. But all thro' the mountains, thunder-riv'n, And up from the rock-y steep,

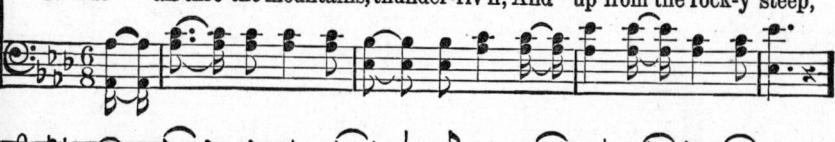

But one was out on the hills a-way, Far-off from the gates of
But the Shep-herd made answer: "This of Mine Has wan-dered a-way from
Nor how dark was the night that the Lord passed thro' Ere He found His sheep that was
'They were shed for one who had gone a-stray Ere the Shepherd could bring him
There a-rose a glad cry to the gate of heav'n, "Re-joice! I have found My

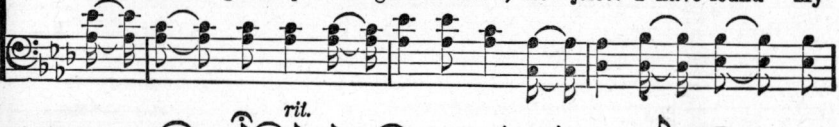

gold— A-way on the moun-tains wild and bare, A-way from the
Me, And al-tho' the road be rough and steep, I go to the
lost. Out in the des-ert He heard its cry— Sick and
back." "Lord, whence are Thy hands so rent and torn?" "They're pierced to-
sheep!" And the an-gels ech-oed a-round the throne, "Re-joice, for the

ten-der Shepherd's care, A-way from the ten-der Shep-herd's care.
des-ert to find My sheep, I go to the des-ert to find My sheep."
helpless, and ready to die; Sick and helpless, and read-y to die.
night by man-y a thorn; They're pierced to-night by man-y a thorn."
Lord brings back His own! Re-joice, for the Lord brings back His own."

196 When the Saints Go Marching In.

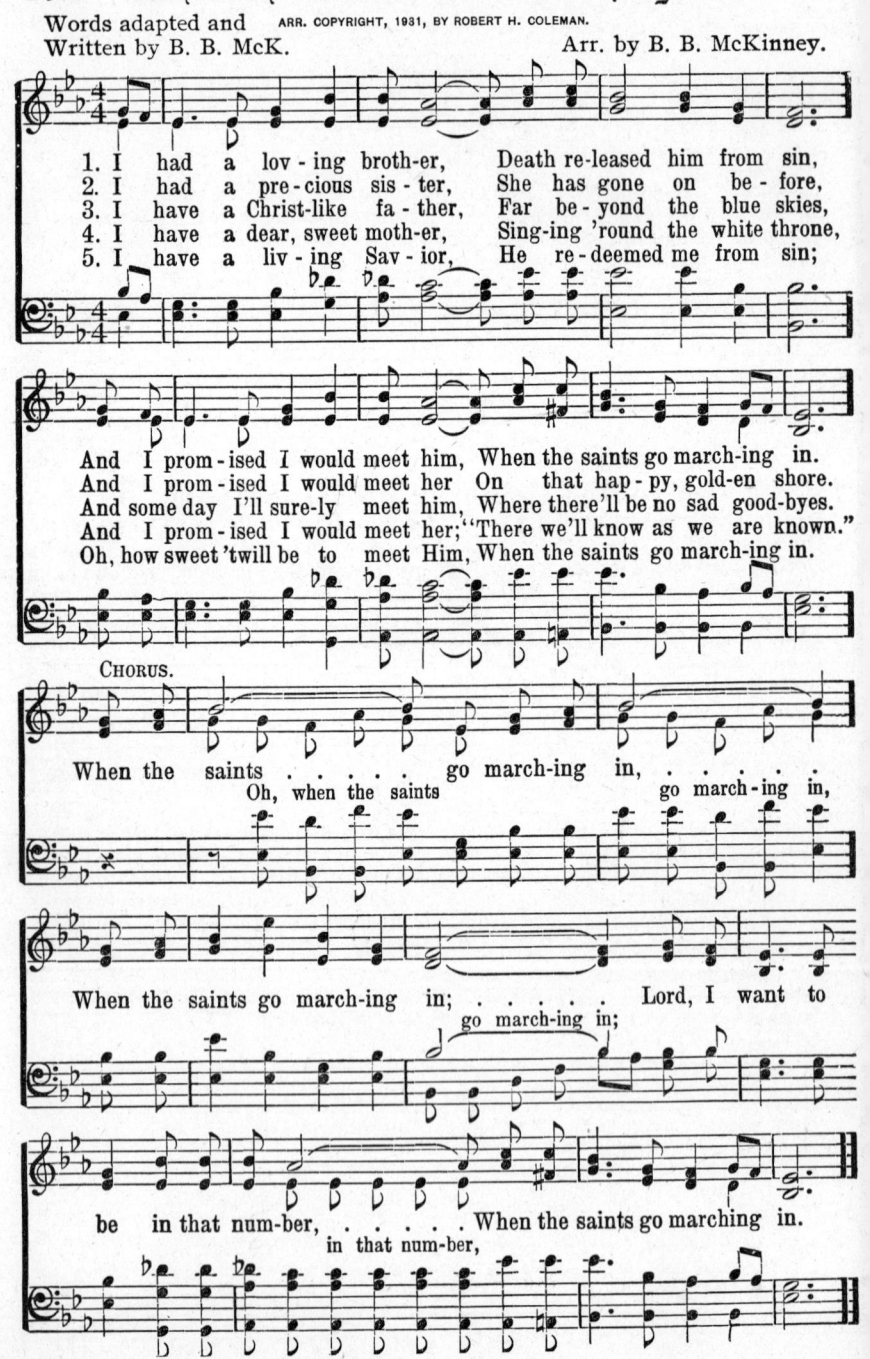

Words adapted and Written by B. B. McK.

ARR. COPYRIGHT, 1931, BY ROBERT H. COLEMAN.

Arr. by B. B. McKinney.

1. I had a lov-ing broth-er, Death re-leased him from sin,
2. I had a pre-cious sis-ter, She has gone on be-fore,
3. I have a Christ-like fa-ther, Far be-yond the blue skies,
4. I have a dear, sweet moth-er, Sing-ing 'round the white throne,
5. I have a liv-ing Sav-ior, He re-deemed me from sin;

And I prom-ised I would meet him, When the saints go march-ing in.
And I prom-ised I would meet her On that hap-py, gold-en shore.
And some day I'll sure-ly meet him, Where there'll be no sad good-byes.
And I prom-ised I would meet her; "There we'll know as we are known."
Oh, how sweet 'twill be to meet Him, When the saints go march-ing in.

CHORUS.

When the saints . . . . . go march-ing in, ...
 Oh, when the saints go march-ing in,

When the saints go march-ing in; . . . . . Lord, I want to
 go march-ing in;

be in that num-ber, ... When the saints go marching in.
 in that num-ber,

INDEX

A Friend to Man.................. 20
A Watchman in the Night....... 70
Abide with Me.................. 69
All thro' the Night..............111
An Eye that Never Sleeps....... 55
Asleep in Jesus.................. 88
Auld Lang Syne..................132

Be a Man....................... 98
Blessed Is He that Readeth......114

Calvary 17
Carry Me Back to Old Virginia..142
Climbing Up Zion's Hill.........131
Come Home 113
Come Unto Me, Ye Weary...... 59
Come, Ye Disconsolate........... 58
Crossing the Bar................143

Day Is Dying in the West....... 37
Dixie Land 149
Don't Forget to Pray............ 41
Down by the Riverside..........123

Fair Eden-land 67
Faith of Our Fathers............140
Father, Hear Us.................112
Fight to Win.................... 74
Four and Twenty Elders.........133

Gathering Home 19
Glorious Things of Thee......... 76
Go thro' the Gates.............. 18
God Be with You................122
God Will Take Care.............108
Going Down the Valley.......... 66
Going Home 50
Going to Shout All Over........124
Goodnight, Ladies 138

Hark! There Comes Whisper.... 89
He Lives on High................ 14
He Loves Me Still............... 7
Hear the Savior's Call........... 1
He'll Keep Me True............. 6
He's Able to Keep You.......... 25
Holy Bible, Book Divine......... 56
Holy Ghost with Light.......... 85
Holy Spirit, Faithful............ 94
Home, Sweet Home..............151
Hush, Somebody's Calling,......126

I Am Safe 49
I Couldn't Hear Nobody.........121
I Know the Lord................127
I Love Him 99
I Shall Not Die................. 28

I Want My Life to Tell.......... 38
In My Heart 137
In the Cross 106
Is Jesus to Me.................. 24
It Came Upon Midnight......... 30
It Is Well with My Soul......... 10

Jesus Calls Us 109
Jesus, Savior, Friend of 65
Jesus, Savior, Pilot Me 79
Jesus, the Light of World....... 47
Jesus, the Very Thought......... 81
Just Outside the Door........... 42

Lead, Kindly Light..............101
Lead Me Gently Home 9
Let the Lower Lights............ 73
Life Is Real....................148
Life's Railway to Heaven........139
List to the Voice................ 68
Looking This Way............... 82

Make Room for Jesus........... 48
May God Depend on You........ 13
Memories of Galilee............. 16
More Love to Thee.............. 97
Must Jesus Bear the Cross....... 77
My Anchor Holds 60
My Anchor Holds Me........... 40
My Country 'Tis of Thee........ 96
My Jesus, I Love Thee.......... 92
My Old Kentucky Home.........145

Nearer Home 80
Nearer, My God, to Thee........ 84
Never Alone 8
Never Grow Old 11
No Burdens Yonder 120
No Night There 44
No Shadows Yonder 119
Now the Day Is Over...........115

O Love that Will Not........... 90
O My Redeemer 5
Old Black Joe 135
Old Folks at Home..............146
One Sweetly Solemn Thought....118
Only Trust in Jesus............. 83
Onward, Christian Soldiers...... 36

Remember Me 71
Rock of Ages................... 86
Rocked in the Cradle of........144
Roll, Billows, Roll.............. 31

Sail On 45
Shall I Crucify Him............. 43

INDEX—Continued

Shall We Meet 104
Shine on Me.................... 46
Silent Night, Holy Night........ 87
Some Morning 105
Some of These Days.............125
Somebody Here Needs Jesus..... 39
Standing in Need of Prayer......134
Stars of Summer Night..........100
Steal Away 136
Sun of My Soul................. 91
Sunset Hour 15
Sweet Bye and Bye.............. 4
Swing Low, Sweet Chariot......128

Tell Me the Old Old Story......116
Tell Mother I'll Be There....... 78
That Beautiful Land............ 72
The Church in Wildwood........ 51
The Day Is Past and Over...... 95
The Face of the Master......... 54
The Haven of Rest.............. 52
The Just Shall Walk............ 57
The Lord Is My Shepherd....... 93
The Many Mansions 107
The Ninety and Nine............ 53
The Old Road 64
The Old Rugged Cross.......... 32

The Riches of Love............. 33
The Royal Telephone 129
The Secret Place 102
The Shadows of the Evening....110
The Star Spangled Banner......147
The Wayside Cross 62
There's No Friend Like Jesus.... 61
Tho' Your Sins Be as Scarlet.... 23
Tramp, Tramp, Tramp..........150
'Twas Jesus' Blood............. 27
Twilight Is Falling............. 75

Under His Wings............... 34

Walk in Jerusalem..............130
Wandering Child, O Come....... 12
We'll Never Say Goodbye........117
What Did He Do................ 63
When I see the Blood........... 29
When the Corn Is Waving.......141
When They Ring Golden Bells... 21
Where We'll Never Grow Old... 26
Where Will You Spend Eternity.103
Will You Come.................. 22
Wonderful Jesus 35
Wonderful Story of Love........ 3

Yield Not to Temptation......... 2

SOLOS, DUETS AND SPECIALS

Back to Bethel..................172
Because 156
Because of You.................169

Crimson Calvary Answers "No"..184

Deep Down in My Heart........168

God Leads Us Along............171
God's Tomorrow 157

He Loves Even Me..............164
He Loves Me 154
He'll Never Forget to Keep Me..176

I Can See the Lights of Home...179
I Walk with the King...........152
I Will Arise and Go to Jesus....191
In the Palace of God's Love.....163

Jesus Is Real and Precious.......173

Leave It There..................161

My Father Watches Over Me....186
My Pilot Will Land the Boat....153

'Neath the Old Olive Trees......159
No Disappointments in Heaven..183

No Shadows Yonder 180
Nothing Between 170

One Day 192
Out of the Deep.................165

Return 185

Satisfied with Jesus.............174
Shadows 181
Softly Now the Light...........189
Some Day It Won't Be Long....175
Sometime 182
Speak to My Heart.............166
Sunrise 158

The Ninety and Nine...........195
The Pearly White City..........188
The Prodigal Son 190
The Wayfaring Pilgrim 178
There Are No Shadows in.......155
Think on Thy Way..............193
This Savior of Mine.............160
'Twill Not Be Long.............162

When the Saints Go Marching...196
Where We'll Never Grow Old....167
Why Should He Love Me So....187
Will the Circle Be Unbroken.....194
Wonderful Love 177